Living Dangerously

Living Dangerously

Seven Keys to Intentional Discipleship

SHAWN D. ANDERSON

WIPF & STOCK · Eugene, Oregon

LIVING DANGEROUSLY
Seven Keys to Intentional Discipleship

Wipf & Stock
An Imprint of Wipf and Stock Publishers
199 W. 8th Ave., Suite 3
Eugene, OR 97401
www.wipfandstock.com

ISBN 13: 978-1-60608-547-9

Manufactured in the U.S.A.

Contents

Figures

Acknowledgments

I AM GRATEFUL FOR many people who have been valuable resources to me in the writing of this book. Several people took time to critique and give valuable suggestions to various parts of the manuscript, including Jason Campbell, Wes Couser, Jane Hess, Dr. Shawn Jones, and Kevin Woods.

Thank you to those who helped in the technical aspects of the manuscript: Michael Morris, who gave my illustrations added flair and zing; Dr. Laurie Walters, who assisted me with statistical analyses; and Dr. John Coffman, who helped shed light on ancient Greek and gave me a better appreciation for biblical languages.

I am also indebted to the colleges and universities that partnered with me in distributing some of the research instruments: Cascade College, George Fox University, Harding University, Ohio Valley College, Rochester College, and York College.

Special thanks goes to Nanette Snipes, who provided expert editing for the entire manuscript.

I am grateful for the members of my church family, the Newberg Church of Christ, who patiently listened to me preach some of the contents in this book.

Finally, thank you to my family and especially my wife, Lisa, who supported me through many hours of writing and was a constant source of encouragement and inspiration.

Introduction

ACCORDING TO A RESEARCH study released in 2009, the church in America is in decline. The number of people who claim to be Christians in the United States has fallen since 1990, from 86 percent to 76 percent.[1] Additionally, the number of people who describe themselves as atheist or agnostic has increased since 1990, from 1 million to 3.6 million.[2]

Why are you reading this book? Perhaps you are concerned about the waning number of Jesus followers, and you are looking for ways to reverse the trend. Possibly you wonder, "Why is my church not doing more to actively reach those who do not know Jesus?" Or, maybe you want to disciple others but do not know where to begin. Whatever the reasons, you are to be commended for taking the initiative and doing something about it.

I have often been struck by the outlook many Jesus followers have toward discipleship. We cannot argue that our responsibility as disciples of Christ is to obey the Great Commission; however, we frequently excuse ourselves from active discipleship. We have been known to say, "It is not my gift," "It is too frightening," or "I don't know how," leaving us with an unanswered, unfulfilled mission.

Realizing that members of the church were not intentionally discipling others, I began searching for the reasons why. I read many books on the needs of unbelievers, and I examined studies that contained massive amounts of data about the spiritual beliefs of unbelievers. I also scrutinized church growth methods and examples in order to learn how to attract others to Jesus. All of my searching was informative, yet something was missing.

One day it dawned on me: My focus should not be on unbelievers—but on me, as a disciple of Jesus! It is not the responsibility of the church to seek and save others, it is mine!

1. Keysar and Kosmin, "American Religious Identification Survey," 3.
2. Keysar and Kosmin, "American Religious Identification Survey," 7.

I determined that I would uncover the mysteries of discipleship by asking people about their conversion process, so I conducted a nation-wide study to better understand how people became followers of Jesus. I hypothesized that people are led to Jesus when there is someone who takes a special interest in their salvation. My thesis was that this person is especially influential in the lives of unbelievers when his or her life reflects Jesus, the greatest teacher of disciples. The results revealed that, indeed, individuals were influenced to commit their lives to Jesus by people who modeled Jesus in their lives.

Knowing that modeling Jesus involves imitating his character traits, I wanted to discover the specific characteristics that influenced unbelievers to give their lives to him. This book reveals those traits, along with the reasons they are important to unbelievers. However, as we will see, simply altering our behaviors does not influence others. We lead people to Jesus when our lives become a reflection of him.

The Great Commission was given to every person who has devoted himself or herself to God. Just as Jesus trained his disciples to disciple others, we have been called to continue the legacy of seeking and saving others. It is not the job of corporate churches or ministers. Jesus has given us—as individual followers of Jesus—the incredible task of discipleship.

Maybe you, like me, desire to know how to disciple others more effectively. What you are about to read is a deliberate wake-up call to discipleship. Turn off the snooze button! It is time for us as individual members of the church to get out of bed and answer God's call to make disciples. This book is a charge to let God take control of our lives by pursuing the Great Commission with passionate zeal. We live dangerously when we intentionally seek others by showing Jesus to them. It is dangerous because discipleship is not an easy calling—it is a life of persecution and rejection. If we sincerely desire to seek and save others, we need to be committed to the process.

The process of discipleship is outlined in this book. Chapters 1 and 2 introduce the concept of living dangerously by modeling Jesus in our lives. Chapter 3 is a brief synopsis of the research study, and portrays an intentional discipler. Chapters 4 through 10 outline the characteristics of an intentional discipler, which also reflect the characteristics of Jesus. Chapter 11 introduces the affiliative model of discipleship and describes how it works. Chapter 12 outlines a plan for discipleship based on the affiliative model, and chapter 13 is a charge for us to live dangerously. Quotes from the research respondents are included in several of the chapters to explain how they were influenced by certain characteristics, and why they felt comfortable discussing spiritual matters. Quotes were lightly edited for grammar, spelling, and punctuation.

Some words used in this book may need clarification:

Unbeliever is used to refer to someone who has not established a relationship with Jesus Christ. An unbeliever is an inclusive term that may refer to someone who was raised going to church but is no longer faithful; it may refer to someone who has little knowledge of Christianity but is open to learning; or an unbeliever may refer to someone who has rejected God. This term is distinguished from the term unchurched, which usually refers to someone who has no church background.

Discipleship is the process of leading someone to Jesus, from being an unbeliever to being in a fully devoted relationship with Jesus. This process involves a mentor who specifically and intentionally guides another person into developing a relationship with Jesus. Discipleship is purposely distinct from evangelism, which is often an ingredient in discipleship, but does not encompass the entire process. Evangelism also has a negative connotation, because we often interpret it as proclaiming mediocre news through coercive methods. For too long, we, as Christians, have focused on evangelism to the detriment of making disciples.

Discipler is a term used to describe someone who actively mentors an unbelieving person into relationship with Jesus and continues to equip the new disciple. This is accomplished by intentionally modeling the characteristics and actions of Jesus, and equipping the disciple through additional teaching.

Disciple refers to people who have committed their lives to be in relationship with Jesus.

Some interpretations and conclusions from the research are offered, but I do not claim to have all the answers. I encourage you to develop your own understanding of the results. Sample discussion questions are included at the end of the chapters to spur thinking in small group or Bible class settings, and encourage you to actively disciple others.

If you are sincere about seeking and saving the lost, this book is for you. Join me on an adventure of becoming an intentional discipler. This book will hopefully challenge you, it may irritate you, but—if you hang with me through it—it will definitely inspire you and give you the tools to disciple others!

The Call to Dangerous Living

If your Gospel isn't touching others, it hasn't touched you!

—CURRY R. BLAKE

ALASKA IS A LAND of extremes. In North Pole, Alaska, where I grew up, the temperature drops to sixty degrees below zero every winter. In this bitter cold, the outside air cannot be inhaled deeply without causing one's lungs to ache, so people often resort to shielding their mouths with scarves. This complicates everyday activities, such as going to the supermarket. Before driving somewhere, one needs to be prepared for the worst-case scenario. For example, vehicles habitually fail to start in the mornings. If a car's oil pan heater is not plugged in overnight, which prevents the engine oil from turning into a thick sludge, there is little chance the vehicle will start. Car batteries frequently die, and require charging or jump-starting. After sitting on ice-covered ground all night, tires freeze on the bottom, giving the sensation of driving on "square" wheels until the tires warm up. If snow accumulation is not cleared from the roads, traveling becomes nearly impossible. Going to the supermarket can easily turn into an all day affair. Winters are also miserably dark. I have memories of riding the bus in total blackness both before and after school. The sun would come up briefly when we were in school, but then only just above the horizon. Summers in Alaska provide a needed respite from the extended winters, although the warmer weather ushers in swarms of mosquitoes, jokingly referred to by the locals as "state birds." Temperatures can reach one hundred degrees, and the sun seems to be permanently suspended in the sky.

Living in this environment is demanding, to say the least. Many people who move to Alaska become weary of the challenging living conditions and leave after a year or two. Only those with mental grit, physical endurance, and determined spirits are able to withstand the inevitable pressures that arise.

Just as residing in Alaska is a commitment to leading an extreme life, followers of Jesus are called to lead extreme lives that are unequivocally devoted to Jesus. In the book of Revelation, the church in Laodicea was prosperous, but smugly self-sufficient. As a result, Jesus warned the church in Revelation 3:15–16: "I know your deeds, that you are neither cold nor hot. I wish you were either one or the other! So, because you are lukewarm—neither hot nor cold—I am about to spit you out of my mouth." In other words, just as both cold and hot water are useful, but lukewarm water is not, Jesus is metaphorically saying that the actions of the Laodicean church were worthless, pointless, and physically nauseating to him.

The words of Jesus have meaning for us today. Jesus does not desire mediocre lives that give lip service; he longs for us to lead a life of extreme hot or cold. If we lead lukewarm lives that are halfheartedly committed to Jesus, he becomes so sickened that he has to spit us out! Sitting on the fence does not cut it; neither does giving 10 percent of our time or resources. We are called to lead lives that are wholly committed to God. He wants all of us!

DISCIPLESHIP 101

How can we lead extreme lives that are totally committed to Jesus? Jesus gave us the answer. Before he ascended to heaven, Jesus gathered his disciples together and charged them with a mission, found in Matthew 28:19–20: "Therefore go and make disciples of all nations, baptizing them in the name of the Father and of the Son and of the Holy Spirit, and teaching them to obey everything I have commanded you. And surely I am with you always, to the very end of the age." This proclamation has been classically coined the "Great Commission," because Jesus is calling us to go and make disciples, regardless of any outside conditions, personal limitations, or external pressures that may threaten our mission. The Great Commission was not only for first century disciples; the charge was also directed toward all subsequent followers of Jesus. We, as heirs of the kingdom of God, are called to follow the Great Commission.

The Greek word translated as "make disciples" in the Great Commission is *matheteusate*, which is the active form of the word for discipleship. It means to teach someone how to acquire a custom or habit. The people who heard Jesus tell them to make disciples had a deep appreciation and understanding of his message, because the concept of discipleship had a rich, traditional meaning. In ancient Judaism, rabbis developed mentoring relationships with their students which involved teaching them Scripture and modeling faithful lives to them. The young apprentices watched and listened to their rabbis closely, until they acquired the customs and habits of their masters. Students of rabbis were commonly referred to as "disciples." Eventually, disciples became copies of their rabbis, and they repeated the process with others.

Just as rabbis sought to reproduce themselves by discipling their students, we are called to make disciples of others. This is accomplished by intentionally developing mentoring relationships with unbelievers and teaching them to acquire the customs and habits of Jesus, the ultimate master.

The Great Commission is comprised of three verbs: go, make disciples, and baptize. In the ancient Greek language, the word for making disciples (matheteusate) is intentionally distinct from the other verbs used in the charge. It is an imperative verb, or a command. In other words, Jesus assumes we are going and baptizing others; but he is specifically commanding us to make disciples. This is not to say that going and baptizing are not important acts—because they are—but that the act of making disciples is the central, highlighted action Jesus calls us to perform.

Making disciples should not be confused with evangelism. In recent years, the definition of evangelism has been expanded to include the process of conversion, but this was not the original meaning of the word. In the ancient Greek language, the active form of evangelism, *euanggelizo*, is typically referred to in the New Testament as proclaiming good news (e.g., Gal 1:8; Rom 10:15; Luke 4:18). Incidentally, this word is not present in the Great Commission. Preaching is often helpful in conversion; but it is not the emphasis of the Great Commission, nor does it always lead to salvation. Jesus expects us to "go" to others, but calls us to spend the bulk of our time making disciples. We have often unwittingly exercised evangelism and evangelistic techniques to the exclusion of making disciples. If implemented correctly, evangelism can be an integral ingredient in discipleship. The distinction is that evangelism does not require us to have personal relationships with people; while making disciples is built upon a foundation of one-on-one relationships.

Discipleship involves creating disciples out of unbelievers. The only other use of the word *matheteusate* in the Bible makes this clear: "When they had preached the gospel to that city and had made many disciples [matheteusate], they returned to Lystra and to Iconium and to Antioch" (Acts 14:21 ESV). The reason that Paul and Barnabas were in Derbe was to convert unbelievers into disciples of Jesus. In the context of the New Testament, a disciple is someone who has decided to follow Jesus and adheres to his teachings.

A brief perusal of biblical scholarship also confirms the conversion aspect of making disciples. The British linguist, F. C. Cook, said making disciples "includes the processes of conversion."[1] Walter Elwell, in his commentary, underscored the two-fold purpose of discipleship. He said, "Discipleship entails both becoming a Christian (being baptized) and being a Christian (obeying Jesus' teaching)."[2] And Gustav Warneck, referred to as the father of Protestant missiology, said that making disciples is "tantamount to making Christians of non-Christians."[3]

Baptism is the third verb mentioned in the Great Commission. Baptism and conversion go hand in hand. In The Expositor's Bible Commentary, Carson said, "The force of the command is to make Jesus' disciples responsible for making disciples of others, a task characterized by baptism and instruction."[4] Baptism should never be left out of the Great Commission. Chapter eleven will explain this act in more detail.

Additionally, the process of making disciples is often mistakenly defined as the task of equipping people who are already believers. Equipping is certainly a critical component of discipleship. After unbelievers have been converted, Jesus instructs us to, "continue teaching them to obey everything I have commanded you" (Matt 28:20). However, if making disciples is restricted to equipping, the process ignores the transforming and converting elements of Jesus' call. In other words, how can we lead people to become disciples if they have already made the decision to follow Christ? Jesus did not say, "Wait until people become believers and then make disciples of them." That would have been redundant and unproductive. Part of our role, as followers of Jesus, is to teach others how to mature in their faith and to prepare them for making disciples of unbelievers.

1. Cook, *The Speaker's Commentary on the New Testament*, 196.
2. Elwell, *Commentary of the Bible*, 760.
3. Warneck, *Evangelische Missionslehre*, 205.
4. Carson, *The Expositor's Bible Commentary*, 597.

Making disciples, baptizing, and teaching are critical components of the Great Commission. However, the charge should not be interpreted as a list of distinctive commands. Rather, the Great Commission is a calling to transform the world through the power and love of Jesus. For the purposes of this book, discipleship is defined as the process of cultivating relationships with unbelievers, mentoring them into developing an intimate, transformative relationship with him, and teaching them to perpetuate the process with others.

This book is a 9-1-1 wake-up call to the mission of making disciples. When we lead people to Jesus, their hearts will bulge with love, their souls will brim with life, and their faces will brighten with light as they come to intimately know him.

A PERSONAL CALLING

The Great Commission is for all those who have committed their lives to Jesus. Notice that Jesus did not add a caveat to his charge: "Make disciples . . . if you have an outgoing personality" or "if it is your gift," or "if you are a minister." While it is true that some people are created with a greater inclination toward making disciples, the apostle Peter reminds us in 2 Peter 2:9 that we are all part of the "royal priesthood." In other words, we are all called to be missionaries to unbelievers. The charge is for anyone striving to follow Jesus—spiritually newborn and mature, poor and rich, male and female, black, white, or any color in between. Obedience to the Great Commission is not an option; it is the reason we follow Jesus. We are all called to be "disciplers."

Making disciples is a personal mission; it is not the job of the church. The church is comprised of many people who have different abilities, talents, and skills, but in the end it is the individual who disciples another person. We cannot hide behind our local congregation and expect it to do the discipling for us. The demanding responsibility of making disciples lies squarely on our shoulders. Jesus said, "As the Father has sent me, I am sending you" (John 20:21). Just as Jesus chose people to disciple personally, we are charged as individuals to disciple others. This may require us to reimagine our church model and faithfully respond to our calling.

Moreover, our goal is not to convert someone to a church, but to Jesus Christ. Membership in a church does not save us or others. Having relationships with other believers is vital to staying spiritually strong;

however, our salvation is contingent upon our relationship with Jesus, expressed through a life of devoted service to God and others. When we lead people to Jesus, our goal is to help them become associated with a gathering of faithful believers. The church becomes their extended family, and the familial relationship blossoms.

UPSIDE-DOWN LIVING

Paul and Silas lived boldly. They were stripped, beaten, and falsely imprisoned. But instead of letting their circumstances deter them from their mission, they converted their jailer and his family. Some of the townspeople in Thessalonica formed a mob and went looking for Paul and Silas. "And when they could not find them, they dragged Jason and some of the brothers before the city authorities, and shouted, "These men who have turned the world upside down have come here also" (Acts 17:6, ESV). The transforming power of Jesus causes people's lives to be turned on their heads. As a result of revolutionary living, Acts 4:4 indicates that the number of Christians in the early church grew to about 5,000—not counting women or children—in an extremely short amount of time.

When we live boldly, people who come to know Jesus are turned upside down by the gospel and their lives will never be the same. They may sacrifice grades, forfeit raises, lose their jobs, or their friends may scatter. Nevertheless, they will come to know Jesus and the amazing love he offers. Organizations will not turn the world upside down; personality will not turn the world upside down; money will not turn the world upside down. Ordinary men and women who love him and trust him to use them will do it. Through the grace of Jesus, when formerly sinful lives are turned upside down they will be given lives of abundance!

Leading lives wholly devoted to the Great Commission is not for the faint of heart or the apathetic—it is dangerous. Being dangerous in this context does not mean leading a life that is hazardous to others. It is defined by living the Great Commission with active passion. It is pushing through the yield signs of fear and complacency that Satan places in our path. Living dangerously is discipling others with reckless abandon, sacrificing our time and energy to show the love of Jesus to others.

A DARING ENDEAVOR

One of the most inspiring accounts of living dangerously is found in the book of Acts. While Peter and John were in Jerusalem, they were taken before the Sanhedrin, the supreme Jewish court, for healing a crippled man in the name of Jesus. When the Sanhedrin cross-examined Peter and John during the proceedings, they did not react out of anxiety or fear; instead, the apostles responded with courage and confidence. This surprised the Sanhedrin, because they knew Peter and John were "unschooled, ordinary men" (Acts 4:13). The Sanhedrin decreed that Peter and John were not allowed to speak or teach in the name of Jesus, to which Peter and John replied, "We cannot help speaking about what we have seen and heard" (Acts 4:20). With very little discussion, the Sanhedrin released Peter and John. Then they joined the other believers in Jerusalem and prayed that God would enable them to speak boldly. Immediately after they finished praying, "they were all filled with the Holy Spirit, and spoke the word of God boldly" (Acts 4:31).

This passage contains some striking examples of dangerous living. Notice that Peter and John never backed down from their beliefs, despite being common fishermen. After they were ordered to stop sharing the gospel of Jesus, they flatly refused. Peter and John knew the Sanhedrin had the power to have them beaten and thrown into prison, yet they chose to continue proclaiming the good news. As fishermen, they had experienced dangerous situations—rough seas and severe weather in a trade that required vigor and physical endurance. Fishing had given Peter and John an inner strength and proven character. Plainly put, Peter and John lived dangerously because they had guts.

Boldness was considered to be such a desirable attribute that Peter and John even asked God to provide it for them, which he did. When our beliefs are under attack or we feel outnumbered, it is natural to be fearful; it is unnatural to be brave. Although Peter and John had faced perilous conditions in their chosen profession, they still depended upon God for courage. When making disciples seems too daring or we are feeling afraid, we can lean on God for support and strength. Prayer gives us the spiritual nourishment we need to live dangerously.

Observe also that Peter and John were common, uneducated men, yet they spoke with such determined authority that the Sanhedrin were stunned. We can learn from this example. Like Peter and John, we do not need to have advanced degrees or a specialized title to disciple others. When we find ourselves in discipling situations that tax our disposition and test our mettle, we can be confident that God is with us, guiding us, and giving us wisdom. The apostle Paul confidently states in Romans 8:31, "If God is for us, who can be against us?" Fishing for men demands absolute reliance upon God.

THE GOSPEL OF DISCOMFORT

Recess was part of the standard schedule in the Alaskan school I attended. However, for six months of the year there was so much snow on the playground that it was impossible to use any of the recreational equipment. For much of the winter, the seats of the swings were virtually at ground level due to the depth of the highly packed snow, which made swinging impractical. See-saws suffered the same fate—the snow was so thick that one could neither teeter, nor totter. So, for a majority of the winter, recesses consisted of my fellow students and I standing huddled together outside with nothing to do except stare blankly at one another.

Further, recess was mandatory until the temperature reached twenty degrees below zero outside. Unfortunately, the average winter temperature in my hometown was fifteen degrees below zero. The only reprieve from the cold was the "warm-up room," a moderately heated room attached to the school building. After waiting in a long line outside, the warm-up room monitors guarding the doors allowed a few of us to come in from the frigid temperatures and sit. As we sat in silence trying to get the blood flowing back into our hands and feet, our minds frequently drifted away to some tropical, faraway place like Tahiti. However, the thawing only lasted a few minutes until the warm-up room monitors ushered us back into the arctic air.

Given the choice, most of us would likely not choose to be freezing in sub-zero weather over lying on a warm, balmy beach. It is human nature to desire comfort and ease. We have grown accustomed to having our homes air-conditioned in the summers and heated in the winters. We coddle ourselves with microwave ovens that prepare dinner in five minutes and television remotes that can change channels without having to get out of our recliners. But living dangerously is not leading a wimpy, lackadaisical existence. Just as the warm-up room monitors would send us back into the cold, Jesus calls us to move beyond our comfort zones by reaching out to unbelievers. We would rather be content in the familiarity of the warm-up room than face the cold unknown of making disciples. Leading a life committed to the gospel is not natural or relaxing; it is uncomfortable. Nevertheless, when others join us in the journey of transformation, we will enjoy basking in the warmth and joy of Jesus together!

The discomfort of the gospel is the realization that the call of Jesus is a purposeful, challenging existence. Discipling others for the cause of Christ can conjure feelings of numbing coldness. If we feel inadequate, anxious, or burdened when we share the good news, we can easily lose our appetites for living dangerously, and will want to quickly return to the safety of the warm-up room to assuage our feelings of fear and doubt. Conversely, if intentionally discipling unbelievers motivates, energizes, and validates our lives, it is a sign that we are completing our task, and the coldness dissipates. This whets our appetites for sharing Jesus with others, and our perspective changes. What was once considered burdensome becomes joyful.

Often, Christians in the church need a jolt of discomforting reality. Those of us who are faithful members will often attempt to satisfy God by agreeing to teach Sunday school, volunteering to be greeters or even using our musical talents as part of the praise team. Do not misunderstand. There is nothing wrong with being an active member of the Lord's body. These acts can do a lot to edify others. However, much of the time we are merely ministering to others who already know Jesus. We get stuck in a church vacuum, because we do not want to leave the spiritual warm-up room called the church. We are exhorted to offer our bodies as "living sacrifices" (Rom 12:1). Making disciples is an act of worship that extends well past the Sunday morning assembly and continues throughout the week. God wants to yank us from our relaxing environments and thrust us into active discipleship.

Without thinking through the implications, we sometimes mistake a comfortable feeling as a Christian virtue. Our comfort becomes the barometer for making spiritual decisions. We might say something such as, "I don't want my kids around unbelievers—they are too rough around the edges," "Talking to people about God makes me uncomfortable," or simply, "I like things the way they are." God has not called us to measure everything according to how we feel; he has called us to stretch ourselves by sharing the gospel with others. Becoming complacent in our faith is a sign that we are not leading the life God intended for us.

Sometimes we attempt to minimize our role in making disciples by shifting our responsibility onto unbelievers. We have often heard churches use the phrase "seeker-sensitive," referring to the mission of the church in the Great Commission. Perhaps we have even seen signs on church billboards proclaim, "Seekers Welcome." The assertion is that unbelievers are the seekers. This is indeed a misnomer because we—as individual disciples of Jesus—are the seekers!

At times, we even want to take the easy way out by nailing banners to the outside of our church buildings or placing advertisements in our local newspapers, expecting unbelievers to flock to our doors. This is wrong, because the Great Commission challenges us—as individual Christians—to go into the world and seek others, not the other way around.

People will not always be receptive to the message of the cross. When we strive to make disciples, we will often be met with resistance, because the gospel does not make sense to unbelievers. In 1 Corinthians 1:23, the apostle Paul acknowledged, "but we preach Christ crucified: a stumbling block to Jews and foolishness to Gentiles." Nevertheless, when people come to truly know Jesus, they experience powerful healing, they are set free from the bondage of sin, and they are given a life of hope!

Jesus did not say that making disciples would be easy. He said in Matthew 16:24, "If anyone would come after me, he must deny himself and take up his cross and follow me." Following Jesus is a demanding, challenging life. This is often referred to as the cost of discipleship. Jesus told us that following him would be hard because he wanted us to be fully devoted to our mission.

Developing relationships with those outside the church walls is uncomfortable; it does not correspond with our traditional church model. We want to maintain the status quo at all costs. But the Great Commission is not a new teaching—it resonates to us as much as it did to those with whom Jesus was speaking. It is time to get out of the warm-up room and develop relationships with those who need God!

Those who choose to live dangerously understand that it will be uncomfortable, but that does not stop them. People who accept this commission are motivated by an internal conviction. They are so overcome with the love of Jesus that his scent infuses the essence of their very being so that every move they make, every word they utter, every breath they breathe exudes the unmistakable sweet fragrance of Jesus, and captures the attention of everyone in the room—both the churched and the unchurched. They are enthralled by the hope of salvation, and it spurs them on to convict others to know the good news.

BURIED TREASURE

What do we do when we find some money in an old pair of pants? Throw it away? Of course not! We celebrate! This is very different from what the man did in the parable Jesus relayed in Matthew 13:44–45: "The kingdom of heaven is like treasure hidden in a field. When a man found it, he hid it again, and then in his joy went and sold all he had and bought that field." Under the Mosaic Law, it was legal to keep something one found—even if it was on someone else's property. The man could easily have kept the treasure for himself. No one would have guessed that the man found the money. Instead, he demonstrated virtuous character by selling his possessions and buying the field.

This is a lesson for us. Jesus has offered himself to us as treasure. Through his sacrifice, we have access to the extraordinary love, strength, wisdom, and daily guidance he offers. For those who do not have a relationship with Jesus, his treasure may as well be buried in a field. These people do not even know the supreme riches available to them. In their search for solutions to the struggles of life, they trample the treasure field every day, unaware of the life-changing benefits buried beneath. People who do not know Jesus do not recognize the value of being in a relationship with him.

We have the treasure map, and it is our mandate to share it with others. Once we have experienced the incomparable blessings of being in a relationship with Jesus, we will no longer desire to keep the treasure to ourselves. We will be so enthralled with the priceless love of Jesus that we will do anything it takes to lead others to him.

In Romans 6:13, the apostle Paul said, "offer yourselves to God." Like the man who sold everything to buy the field with the hidden treasure, responding to the Great Commission requires a life that is sacrificially dedicated to God. When we are thoroughly consumed with discipling others our lives will be a sweet-smelling fragrance to God.

Living dangerously makes about as much sense as burying riches in a can, and then selling everything we have to buy it back. Why would we willingly make our lives uncomfortable? Why would we choose to do something difficult like giving away everything to pursue the Great Commission? It is because Jesus called us to sacrifice our lives to God because he first sacrificed his life for us. God called us to surrender to him by guiding others into relationship with him. God is depending on us to reveal his hidden treasure!

LIVING DANGEROUSLY

This chapter was intended to challenge your thinking and stir you to action. Perhaps it even angered you a little. That is okay, because making disciples is the most difficult job in the universe. It is daring, uncomfortable, and difficult. However, Jesus did not give you the charge and then leave you desolate—he knew you could handle it, and he gives you the spiritual fortitude and strength to accomplish your mission.

If your life as a follower of Jesus is not thoroughly and intensely dedicated to making disciples, this book is for you. Ask yourself who you know that needs the treasure of salvation. Your mission is to lead that person to Jesus. He is waiting with open arms to give this person spiritual wealth. Do not let your friend walk on the field with riches beneath his feet. Do not withhold spiritual blessings from him. Pray for him. Ask God to prepare you to live dangerously and share his treasure with others. I pray that the Holy Spirit will guide you as you fulfill your greatest calling.

QUESTIONS FOR DISCUSSION

- What is something you have accomplished that was extremely difficult to do? Why did you do it?

- Explain why Jesus wants us to be hot or cold, but not lukewarm. How does this fit with what the apostle Paul said in Romans 12:1?

- Why do people sometimes view the charge to make disciples as the task of the church or the hired minister instead of everyone's job? How can we help change this perception?

- In what ways does the gospel of Jesus turn the lives of unbelievers upside down, as mentioned in Acts 17:1-6?

- Read Matthew 16:24. Why would Jesus charge us to do something that is out of our comfort zones?

PERSONAL REFLECTION

- Are you answering the call to make disciples? If not, what can you do differently?

- Think of someone you know who needs the transforming power of Jesus. Ask God for wisdom to know the best way to share the good news with this person.

2

The World's Most Dangerous Man

Jesus, like any good fisherman,
first catches the fish; then He cleans them.

—MARK POTTER, BRITISH COURT JUDGE

WHEN I WAS GROWING up, the Tanana River in Alaska was primarily where my family spent our recreation time. We would fish in the river, explore its vast tributaries, and camp by the river's edge. Many enjoyable childhood memories of mine were formed here. One particularly memorable incident happened on the Tanana when I was eight years old. My family had an opportunity to stay overnight in a rustic cabin by the river, so we packed for the night and launched our boat in the river. After we arrived and began unpacking our gear, my father asked me if I wanted to take a "nature hike" into the woods. He began showing me signs of wildlife, such as rabbit tracks, moose droppings, and bear scat. The sightseeing tour took us deeper into the woods, and when we decided to return to camp, we ended up going in the wrong direction. We soon realized that we were lost. To make matters worse, we had no food, water, proper clothing, or a compass. We sustained ourselves by drinking muddy river water and eating wild blueberries, cranberries, and blackberries. At one point, we spotted a cabin on the other side of a small tributary. My father put me on his shoulders and carefully walked through the chilly waters. When we reached the middle of the river, I vividly remember the flowing water swirling around my father's chin. When we arrived at the other side of the river, we realized that the cabin had been boarded up and abandoned. However, we found an old canoe and floated downstream for a couple of hours. By this time it was getting late, the night fog was rolling in, and we were miles downstream from our camp, even though my father did recognize where we were. We decided to stop and rest for the night. I constructed a bed of leaves to help protect myself from the cold ground and slept. I do not remember my father sleeping that night. The next morning we heard a motorboat in the distance. As the boat drew nearer, we noticed there were two military soldiers conducting survival training exercises. They greeted us and graciously offered to give us a ride back to our camp.

Being physically lost is unpleasant, frustrating, tiresome, fearful, and panicking. Being spiritually lost conjures similar feelings, except that as disciples of Jesus, we have already been found. If we can recall being spiritually lost, we also likely remember how amazing and spectacularly refreshing it felt to finally find Jesus. Jesus has already shown us the way to salvation. Like the men in the riverboat, Jesus knew his mission well, and he was singularly focused in his actions. He declared in Luke 19:10, "For the Son of Man came to seek and to save what was lost." Jesus spent his life conducting spiritual training exercises, and he provided direction to everyone he met so that they too could seek and save the lost. Jesus is our spiritual compass. He will never make us row upstream without a paddle because he loves us completely. Jesus provides spiritual food to sustain us, living water that will forever quench our thirst, and arms that provide a safe resting place.

AN AUDACIOUS SAVIOR

People who have not encountered Jesus often presume he is a wimpy, milquetoast Savior who is unable or unwilling to significantly make a difference in their lives. This is not the Savior I know. Jesus threw caution to the wind. He often willingly and fearlessly put himself in jeopardy. Jesus was the most intentional discipler who ever lived. In three short years, he introduced and implemented a gospel that revolutionized the world. Beginning with a motley group of twelve men, the gospel of Jesus Christ has exploded exponentially into becoming the world's largest religion. How did Jesus do it? His beliefs were unshakable and he was unequivocally committed to completing his mission on earth. He was the world's most dangerous man!

Jesus was dangerous because he was not afraid to say and do what he believed, regardless of the potential outcome. For instance, in the Gospel of John, the Pharisees accused Jesus of being demon-possessed. The discussion ended when Jesus fearlessly stated in John 8:58, "before Abraham was born, I am!" When Jesus said those words, it incited the Pharisees to try and stone him. Why did these particular words inflame the Pharisees to this extent? From the time they were children, Jews were trained in their nation's history, and this history was deeply intertwined with their faith. They knew that God advised Moses to tell the Israelites, "I am has sent me to you" (Exod 3:14). By saying "before Abraham was born, I am," Jesus was unmistakably equating himself with God. To the Pharisees, this was pure blasphemy! Of course Jesus knew they felt this way, but he was willing to risk his life by plainly speaking the truth!

Jesus lived so boldly that he ended up breaking sacred traditions. Luke records a time when Jesus entered a synagogue on the Sabbath and saw a man with a shriveled hand. Luke 6:7–11 says:

> The Pharisees and the teachers of the law were looking for a reason to accuse Jesus, so they watched him closely to see if he would heal on the Sabbath. But Jesus knew what they were thinking and said to the man with the shriveled hand, "Get up and stand in front of everyone." So he got up and stood there. Then Jesus said to them, "I ask you, which is lawful on the Sabbath: to do good or to do evil, to save life or to destroy it?" He looked around at them all, and then said to the man, "Stretch out your hand." He did so, and his hand was completely restored. But they were furious and began to discuss with one another what they might do to Jesus.

Jesus was well aware of the trap that the Pharisees and teachers of the law were trying to set for him, but he ignored their concerns and fearlessly healed the man. To Jesus, people were more important than traditions.

These examples unmistakably demonstrate the courageous life that Jesus led. He was so passionate about his purpose and so intentionally engrossed in making disciples that he often incited people to defensiveness or anger, but he was never tempted to dilute his message. He was convicted of his message, he was brutally honest, and he did not cave to political pressures or personal preferences. Everything Jesus did was related to making disciples—from teaching to performing miracles. He lived audaciously, and he did not allow anyone to get in the way of his mission.

It is time to ask ourselves some tough questions. Are we, like Jesus, living audacious lives? Perhaps we faithfully attend worship services, are involved in several church ministries, and even read our Bibles every day. These are all commendable actions, but they do not make disciples. We may feel spiritually close to Jesus, but keep the joy of the cross to ourselves. If this is the case, something needs to change. Jesus did not come to enforce rituals, customs, or ancient sacrifices. He said, "I desire mercy, not sacrifice" (Matt 9:13). Jesus is calling us to live audaciously by sharing our joy with unbelievers and lead them to him.

MODEL BEHAVIOR

A disciple is someone who emulates the behavior and actions of someone else until she actually becomes a different person. In the sixth century BC, there lived a Scythian philosopher named Anacharsis. Although the Scythians hated the Greeks, Anacharsis fell in love with Greek life. He traveled to Greece and decided to imitate Greek culture—he learned the language, he wore Greek clothing, he ate Greek food, he worshipped Greek gods, and he decorated his palace with Greek art. He became so consumed with the culture that Anacharsis was sometimes mistaken for a Greek. When Anacharsis returned home, his countrymen told him that he was not only like a Greek, but had actually become a Greek—and they killed him.[1]

Just as Anacharsis imitated Greek culture until he was indistinguishable from a Greek; we, as disciples of Jesus, will be transformed into his image when we are consumed with emulating him. This is the essence of the message Paul is conveying in 2 Corinthians 3:18: "And we, who with unveiled faces all reflect the Lord's glory, are being transformed into his likeness with ever-increasing glory, which comes from the Lord, who is the Spirit." If we emulate the life of Jesus, the master discipler, we will become more like him every day. This is a lifelong process; it does not happen overnight. This transformative process is made possible through the Holy Spirit. His power guides us and changes us into the image of Jesus Christ. Our calling is to become a clone of Jesus—without fear of ethical implications.

When we are transformed into his likeness, others will see Jesus in us and come to know the power that shatters fears and doubts and gives them hope. In 1 Corinthians 11:1, the apostle Paul beckons: "Follow my example, as I follow the example of Christ." There is no better model for

1. Herodotus. *The Histories*, 4.76.

making disciples than Jesus! He taught his followers how to disciple others by modeling his life for them—and it worked. Teaching others to blindly follow a list of hollow rules or mindlessly alter their actions to match a set of preconceived expectations does not change hearts and souls. As followers of Jesus, our role is to learn how to make disciples through the example of Jesus and then intentionally lead others in their own transformative process.

It is only possible to make disciples if our lives have been spiritually transformed. Paul told the Corinthian church in 2 Corinthians 5:17–18: "Therefore, if anyone is in Christ, he is a new creation; the old has gone, the new has come! All this is from God, who reconciled us to himself through Christ and gave us the ministry of reconciliation." When we make the decision to follow Jesus, he makes us compatible with him by spiritually changing us. The Holy Spirit ensures that conversion is not merely a change of outward actions, but is a metamorphosis of our entire being from sinfulness to Christlikeness.

Just as a caterpillar is transformed into a beautiful butterfly, God's intention is to transform us by wrapping us in his love, feeding us through his Word, and changing us from the inside out to reflect the glory of Jesus! This means that when others see us they do not notice our weaknesses and faults—they see a reflection of Jesus in us. This transformation was made possible by God sending Christ to die for us, so we could be made right before God. Since we have been reconciled to God, we have been charged with the ministry of reconciliation by bringing others to him.

COVENANT RELATIONSHIP

God desired to be in a relationship with us from the beginning. This is made evident by a casual reading of the creation narrative: "Let us make man in our image, in our likeness" (Gen 1:26). God also established a special relationship with the nation of Israel. He said, "Now if you obey me fully and keep my covenant, then out of all nations you will be my treasured possession" (Exod 19:5). Despite this covenantal relationship, Israel turned her back on God many times. Nevertheless, God always accepted her back. Likewise, God never turns his back on us because he is in relationship with us.

We can be in relationship with God because he sent Jesus to earth to live as a man. John said in John 1:14: "The Word became flesh and made his dwelling among us. We have seen his glory, the glory of the One and Only, who came from the Father, full of grace and truth." Jesus came in the flesh so that we might be in relationship with him. Because of his life and sacrifice, we are still able to be in relationship with him! Jesus is not just in relationship with us; he is part of us and wants to be manifested through us. The Master of the universe desires to be close to us!

DANGEROUS LIAISONS

Jesus also desired to intimately know unbelievers. He had a secret weapon in making disciples—relationship. Jesus was the kind of person who would jump into a shark-infested tank to save a minnow from being eaten. Why? He was consumed with loving others and desired to demonstrate that love by being in relationship with people.

Jesus especially sought to be in relationship with those who were poor, lame, and spiritually sick. Jesus called to these people in Matthew 11:28: "Come to me, all you who are weary and burdened, and I will give you rest." We can learn a lot about discipling others by examining Jesus' relationships with people. His discipling plan included identifying people with deep spiritual needs, and then satisfying those needs. Many times, those people were shunned by others because they were considered undesirable.

On one such occasion Jesus had dinner with Levi, who was despised because he was a tax collector. Mark notes this event in Mark 2:15–17: "While Jesus was having dinner at Levi's house, many tax collectors and 'sinners' were eating with him and his disciples, for there were many who followed him. When the teachers of the law who were Pharisees saw him eating with the 'sinners' and tax collectors, they asked his disciples: 'Why does he eat with tax collectors and sinners?' On hearing this, Jesus said to them, 'It is not the healthy who need a doctor, but the sick. I have not come to call the righteous, but sinners.'"

The reason Jesus spent time with the outcasts of society is because no one else wanted them. Social mores justified ignoring them, discriminating against them, and treating them with contempt. Jesus came to offer them love and healing. He treated them with respect and dignity. This mission is evident in his Sermon on the Mount, from Matthew 5:3-6:

- Blessed are the poor in spirit, for theirs is the kingdom of heaven.

- Blessed are those who mourn, for they will be comforted.

- Blessed are the meek, for they will inherit the earth.

- Blessed are those who hunger and thirst for righteousness, for they will be filled.

Jesus rescued people from their infirmities because he was the Great Physician. He intentionally desired to have dangerous liaisons, leaving his critics with eyes wide and mouths agape.

Jesus was not content with having superficial relationships; he desired to know people intimately. When Jesus met people, he dug into their psyches and addressed their deepest concerns. For example, Jesus intentionally sought to heal the deep spiritual yearnings of a wealthy tax collector named Zacchaeus. Zacchaeus was despised by the residents of Jericho because he was considered to be deceitful and contemptuous. When Jesus visited Jericho, Zacchaeus climbed up a tree to see above the crowd that had gathered. As soon as Jesus saw him, he said, "Zacchaeus, come down immediately. I must stay at your house today" (Luke 19:5). How did the townspeople react? Luke 19:7 says, "All the people saw this and began to mutter, 'He has gone to be the guest of a 'sinner.'"

By becoming acquainted with Zacchaeus, Jesus opened the door for conversion to occur. This was a dangerous thing to do because Jesus risked being rejected by the people. He was able to look past Zacchaeus's sin and quench his spiritual hunger.

Another time, Jesus was invited to have dinner with a Pharisee and ended up encountering a prostitute. The woman wet Jesus' feet with her tears, wiped them with her hair, kissed them, and anointed them with oil. Seeing that Jesus allowed the woman to do these things, Simon questioned Jesus' actions in Luke 7:39: "If this man were a prophet, he would know who is touching him and what kind of woman she is—that she is a sinner." In Jesus' day, just talking to a prostitute made a person unclean. Instead of condemning the woman or simply ignoring her, Jesus forgave her sins! Simon must have come unglued! Associating with a prostitute—let alone blessing one—was a completely foreign idea.

Luke does not tell us what happened to the prostitute after she encountered Jesus. We have all heard preachers speculate that she went away a transformed woman, but it is also plausible that she completely walked away from Jesus. If this happened, it lends credence to the idea that building relationships with unbelievers is dangerous. We are called to disciple people regardless of how well they respond to the gospel or how often we are criticized by others. Jesus calls us, as individuals, to be dangerous disciplers. And sometimes that results in failure.

When we find others with needs, Jesus invites us to partner with them in meeting those needs by intentionally entering into relationships with them. Sometimes relationships fail to impact people spiritually; other times, relationships blossom into full-blown discipling relationships and people are led to Jesus.

If Jesus were on the earth today, how would he find people to disciple? He would go to them! Since Jesus ate with tax collectors and sinners and befriended prostitutes, would it be a stretch to suggest that in our time he would go to places like bars and casinos? This may be a difficult concept to swallow, but considering that Jesus came to meet the needs of the sick, would it seem feasible that he would spend most of his time in churches? Likewise, we need to go and disciple people who have needs.

What can we learn from the actions of Jesus? We need to have a spiritual yearning to seek the lost. Before Jesus enters Jerusalem for the last time, Luke records that he looked over the city and cried out, "O Jerusalem, Jerusalem, you who kill the prophets and stone those sent to you, how often I have longed to gather your children together, as a hen gathers her chicks under her wings, but you were not willing!" (Luke 13:34). Jesus was weeping for those who would not accept him. At the brink of his crucifixion, he was more concerned for the lost in Jerusalem than for his own suffering! Do we feel this sense of compassion for the lost? If not, it is time for us to be like Jesus. First, we need to get off our complacent duffs and take our calling seriously. Second, we must intentionally strive to have relationships with hurting people, realizing that we may not necessarily lead them to Jesus. Finally, we must be willing to sacrifice everything—even ourselves—to make disciples.

FISHING LESSONS

Have you ever stopped fishing because it was too easy? I had this experience—once. It happened to me several years ago when I was fishing off the coast of Alaska for halibut. My group chartered a boat and set course for a few miles outside of Sitka. Instead of letting us make common fishing mistakes, the leader of the group took time to demonstrate to us the proper technique of fishing for halibut. He made sure the boat's anchor was set, and then he weighted his fishing line and dropped it all the way to the ocean floor. Then, since halibut swim near the bottom of the ocean, he reeled his line in a couple of feet and waited. We watched and learned. As I was preparing my fishing pole and bait, another member of our group let down his line and almost immediately felt a bite. He pulled in a nice, medium-sized halibut! Anxious to try, I dropped my line and, to my amazement, the same thing happened to me! Was this a fluke? I dropped my line again, and within seconds, I got another bite. It was too much fun! In no time, we all had caught our limit.

Like the fishing guide, Jesus came to teach people how to fish—not for halibut—but for men. He began his mission when he approached, ironically enough, two fishermen named Peter and Andrew. Matthew 4:19 records that Jesus told them, "Come, follow me," "and I will make you fishers of men." Just as our leader demonstrated the best method of fishing for halibut, Jesus dedicated three years of his life instructing his followers how to make disciples of those who were spiritually lost.

Jesus not only discipled others, but he continued the cycle by giving fishing lessons to his followers. Through his example and teachings, he passed on valuable lessons of discipleship. His disciples learned well, and the cycle was perpetuated through subsequent generations.

Essentially, our role is to introduce people to Jesus. We can do this by cultivating within others an appreciation for who he is and what he has done in our lives. If we intentionally model Jesus in our lives and spend time discipling others, the Holy Spirit will guide them into developing a deep, abiding relationship with Jesus. When people are drawn into the warm embrace of God, his love washes over them, and they are changed on the inside. This inward transformation radiates from their hearts and is brought to fruition by leading lives that look like Jesus.

OUR DANGEROUS MISSION

Jesus was able to successfully influence others because he knew where he was going. After the Pharisees told Jesus he could not testify about himself, he replied in John 8:14, "Even if I testify on my own behalf, my testimony is valid, for I know where I came from and where I am going." Jesus' goal was to seek and save the lost, and his eyes were resolutely focused on finishing that race. He allowed nothing to throw him off course.

Likewise, we need to know where we are going in our spiritual walk. What is our mission as disciples of Jesus? To be intentional disciplers, our mission needs to be firmly established. How can we lead others if we do not know where we are headed? Many unbelievers do not have spiritual direction. If we are confused about our faith, we are incapable of leading them to Jesus. Jesus entrusted us to transform the world with his message. Second Corinthians 5:20 says we are Christ's ambassadors, meaning that we represent Jesus and we speak for him. We need to decide what our ultimate purpose for living is—and then act on it! Like Jesus, this takes total devotion to our calling, letting nothing distract us from leading others to the finish line of salvation.

This awesome responsibility requires us to prioritize our discipling efforts. A life committed to making disciples demands us to place God first, and relegate everything else to second place. Observe these challenging words of Jesus from Matthew 10:34–39:

> Do not suppose that I have come to bring peace to the earth. I did not come to bring peace, but a sword. For I have come to turn "a man against his father, a daughter against her mother, a daughter-in-law against her mother-in-law—a man's enemies will be the members of his own household." Anyone who loves his father or mother more than me is not worthy of me; anyone who loves his son or daughter more than me is not worthy of me; and anyone who does not take his cross and follow me is not worthy of me. Whoever finds his life will lose it, and whoever loses his life for my sake will find it.

Jesus was not saying that our families are unimportant, and he is not saying that choosing to follow him invariably causes our loved ones to run away from us. Caring for our families is a command from the Lord, but following Jesus takes priority. Living for Jesus means placing him first in everything we do.

If we choose to follow the example of Jesus, we will never demote him to the backseat; or, for that matter, be comfortable with him as our co-pilot. Living dangerously means leading a life that is totally surrendered to him.

Having a mission gives us a distinctive purpose and a hungry passion for living. If our mission in life is clearly defined, it will be intertwined throughout our very being, and will be expressed through our thoughts and actions. A mission gives our life meaning. If we spend our entire lives performing routine acts of eating, working, sleeping—even going to church—our lives have no more significance than a grain of sand on the vast seashore.

Thinking about our mission can be scary and extremely unsettling. Many of us have established a pattern of living that is relaxed and demands very little energy. We dislike interruptions to our routine, we are often selfish with our time, and we tend to ignore people who do not promote our own self interests. We want things to remain the same, and we will typically fight anything that may potentially threaten our familiar lifestyle. This is not living dangerously; it is simply survival. If we are going through the motions of self-preservation, then we are effectively tranquilizing ourselves into spiritual slumber.

Jesus is calling us to a far greater life. He wants to rouse us from our mundane existence with the smelling salts of a dangerously centered life. Moreover, he wants others to be mesmerized by his fragrance in our lives.

How can we lead unbelievers to drink from the abundant, fulfilling wellspring of life that Jesus offers? We need to ask ourselves what we can do differently that will break the mission-less cycle of living—and then do it!

THE CHALLENGE TO LIVE LIKE JESUS

Jesus was—and still is—the world's most dangerous man. He brazenly lived his mission, despite possible repercussions; he sought others who had needs, even if they were looked down upon by their own people; and he taught his followers how to make disciples so well that the cycle continues today. Our mandate is to follow the example Jesus set for us. We may be the only link between someone else and him! When our lives reflect the character of Jesus, his love will naturally compel others to follow him.

Are you modeling Jesus in your life? Do others see Jesus reflected in you? If they do not, Jesus is calling you to repent by transforming your life to reflect his glory. Socrates said, "The unexamined life is not worth living." An undefined life has a definite purpose—but it is certainly not following Jesus! Jesus has charged you to make disciples by modeling him in your life. Will you accept your mission?

QUESTIONS FOR DISCUSSION

- Have you ever been lost? Describe your experience.

- Second Corinthians 3:18 says that we are in the process of being transformed into the likeness of Jesus. What does this look like?

- Read Luke 19:10. Why is it dangerous to have the same mission as Jesus?

- Why is relationship important in discipling others?

- Can you imagine yourself interacting with the kinds of people that Jesus did? What are some ways you can intentionally develop relationships with people who are spiritually hungry?

PERSONAL REFLECTION

- Outside of church, work, school, meals, and sleep, how do you spend your time? Is this an indication of your mission as a disciple of Jesus?

- Pray that God will show you how he can use you for his purposes.

3

Profile of an Intentional Discipler

Discipleship means adherence to the person of Jesus, and therefore submission to the law of Christ which is the law of the cross.

—DIETRICH BONHOFFER

WHAT IS THE FIRST thing you think of when someone says Alaska? People often have misunderstandings about the Last Frontier. When I mention to people that I grew up in North Pole, Alaska, I get asked all sorts of questions. Did you live in an igloo? Does it stay dark for six months out of the year? If you throw a glass of water up in the air at fifty degrees below zero, does it freeze before it hits the ground? Did you travel by dogsled? The answer to these questions is negative, but it would be difficult to know these things unless one had lived in Alaska.

Alaskans also have their own peculiar vernacular. If we say we are going outside for the winter, it does not mean sleeping with the polar bears, it means traveling to the contiguous United States; if we say someone is a sourdough, it does not mean that person has a bad attitude, it means he has survived an Alaskan winter and decided to stay; if someone talks about a spring breakup, she is not referring to a relationship that did not work out, but the time of year when the snow and ice melts.

Just as some U.S. citizens have misconceptions of Alaska, a number of Christians have false impressions of disciplers. Some say that disciplers are born—not made—and will blame their laziness on a shortage of evangelistic gifts. Others assume that disciplers have magnetic, outgoing personalities that easily attract people to them. Still other believers misunderstand the process of making disciples entirely by limiting it to a series of hierarchical steps, or by viewing the process as completed when the other person commits her life to Jesus.

A REVELATION

A few years ago, I began to realize there are lots of misconceptions regarding disciplers and the process of making disciples. I became frustrated with the efforts my church put into reaching unbelievers—they simply did not work. We transformed our worship services, we instituted all kinds of programs and ministries, and we even began offering bilingual services to reach Spanish-speaking people. Our church had honorable intentions, but we were clearly not converting many others to Jesus.

What were we doing wrong? Nothing—except that our focus was off! We were trying to reach people without getting to know them. Our emphases were based on corporate marketing approaches and impersonal appeals. I also came to realize that the church—as an institution—is not responsible for saving others. I realized I needed to do something to reverse this trend. Jesus was calling me, so I decided to take the initiative and do something different!

In an effort to understand the process of conversion more fully and equip myself spiritually, I desperately devoured books and articles written about reaching others. Some of my reading focused on the characteristics of unbelievers: who they are, what they think about Christianity, and what beliefs they hold. Further exploration revealed detailed evangelistic methods or practices that were downright complicated. Some of the information I read was helpful, but I was often left with a feeling of inadequacy. After spending much time in prayer, a revelation occurred to me: if I wanted to be an effective discipler, I would need to find out how I could lead someone to Jesus by working on myself—how to grow spiritually and how to become more like Jesus.

To understand what characteristics Jesus had that I could emulate, I decided to ask other disciples of Christ about their conversion process. Was there someone who was influential in their conversion? If so, what was the relationship they had with the person? Who brought up Jesus first in conversation? What characteristics of Jesus did that person possess that prompted them to commit their lives to him? How long did the conversion process take?

These were some of the questions that were burning in my mind. I decided to ask people about their conversion process by having them answer these questions. A nationwide research study was conducted to discover what influenced them to follow Jesus. The goal was to discover how to be an intentional discipler.

Perhaps you—like me—want to become an intentional discipler. You desire to dangerously share the good news, but you are not sure how to do it. You may be desperately searching for resources that can better equip you to disciple others. As the results of the research are revealed to you, ask yourself what the data show you about yourself: how is an intentional discipler like or unlike you, and what can you do to strengthen your ability to make disciples?

Is there someone who is especially influential in leading unbelievers to Jesus? Seventy percent of those surveyed said there was someone who was influential in leading them to Jesus (see figure 3.1). We can conclude with a high degree of confidence that an overwhelming majority of people who were led to Jesus had a relationship with another person who discipled them through the process of conversion. This person will be referred to as a "discipler." There may have been other factors that contributed to the conversion process, such as church or personal Bible study, but the overriding reason people were led to Jesus was because they had a relationship with someone who intentionally discipled them.

Figure 3.1
Was there someone who was especially influential in leading you to Jesus?

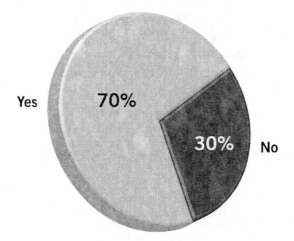

CHARACTERISTICS OF AN INTENTIONAL DISCIPLER

Disciplers who are intentional in leading people to Jesus have certain defining characteristics. People who indicated there was someone especially influential in leading them to Jesus were asked to describe that person. Figure 3.2 indicates that 61 percent of disciplers were male and 39 percent were female. Does this mean that men are more effective disciplers than women? Not necessarily. As someone who has taught statistics, I realize how easy it is to jump to conclusions with quantitative data. The data simply illustrate that the majority of disciplers in the study were male. We will correlate gender to other factors in later chapters.

Figure 3.2
What gender is the person who was influential in leading you to Jesus?

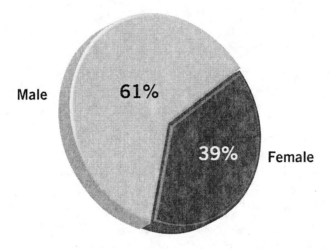

The age of the discipler is another demographic piece that is useful to examine. Former unbelievers were asked to reveal the age of the person who was influential in their conversion. The options were age groups which had been identified as generationally distinct. Figure 3.3 shows disciplers in the study as categorized by age groups. Forty-eight percent of disciplers were between twenty-nine and forty-three years old. This was higher than any other age group. The remaining 52 percent were comprised of other age groups. Twenty-five percent of disciplers were between fourteen and twenty-eight years of age, 22 percent were forty-four to sixty-two years old, and 4 percent of disciplers were sixty-three years old and older. Interestingly, no disciplers were below thirteen years of age.

Figure 3.3
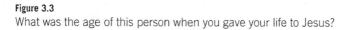
What was the age of this person when you gave your life to Jesus?

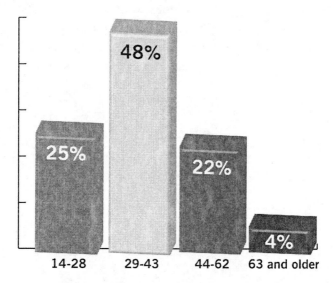

A discipler cannot influence an unbeliever unless the two have a relationship. To discover what kind of relationship influenced an unbeliever, former unbelievers were asked to describe the relationship that influenced them to follow Jesus. Fifty-two percent indicated that a relative had the greatest influence on them (see figure 3.4). This was no surprise, because it validated the findings of previous research studies.[1] Friends were named by 20 percent of those who were unbelievers, and 18 percent said ministers had the greatest influence on them. The remaining 10 percent of relationships that influenced unbelievers—although to much lesser degrees—were neighbors, coworkers, Bible teachers, professors, camp counselors, youth interns, and even a few homeless people! The low preponderance of neighbors and coworkers was particularly astonishing, since many programs designed to make disciples emphasize sharing the

---

1. Rainer, *Surprising Insights From the Unchurched,* 48; Barna, *Evangelism Is Most Effective Among Kids,* §5.

gospel in these kinds of relationships. This could mean several things: 1) we have tried to disciple neighbors and coworkers but they have rejected our advances; 2) we have not been adequately equipped to reach them; 3) we have simply been afraid to share the gospel with them; or 4) it is much easier to influence relatives than neighbors or coworkers.

Figure 3.4
What was your relationship with this person when you first met?

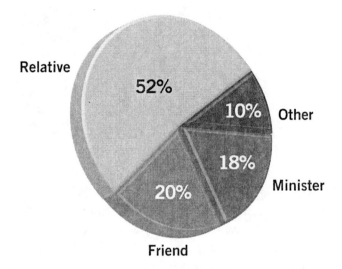

Since relationships are crucial to making disciples, it would be helpful to know how long people were involved in these relationships before Jesus was mentioned in conversation. Forty-eight percent of those who were unbelievers acknowledged they had a relationship with a discipler three months or less before Jesus was brought up in conversation (see figure 3.5). The second most common length of time before Jesus came up in conversation was over a year. This was asserted by 42 percent of respondents. Only 5 percent of those who were unbelievers indicated that it took four to six months or six months to a year before Jesus was introduced in conversation.

Figure 3.5
How long did you know this person before Jesus came up in conversation?

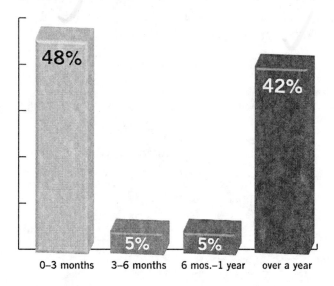

| 0–3 months | 3–6 months | 6 mos.–1 year | over a year |

Who was the one who brought up Jesus first in the relationship? Eighty-four percent of the time, disciplers were the initiators (see figure 3.6). There have been many debates over who should initiate conversations about Jesus. Should we, as disciplers, be the first ones to bring up spiritual matters? Will the other person close his or her mind to future conversations about Jesus if we bring up Jesus too early in the relationship? One of the prevailing ideas is that if we are living like Jesus, the other person will eventually initiate spiritual conversations. However, the research showed just the opposite: we, as intentional disciplers, need to initiate spiritual discussions.

Figure 3.6
Which one of you was the first person to bring up Jesus in conversation after you met?

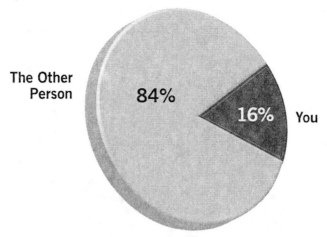

Once Jesus was brought up in a discipling relationship, how long did it take for an unbeliever to give her life to Jesus? Fifty-one percent of the time this process took over a year (see figure 3.7). It took 25 percent of unbelievers three months or less to give their lives to Jesus, and 15 percent of them took from six months to a year to give their lives to him. Only 9 percent gave their lives to Jesus between four and six months. It is intriguing that the discipling process took so long. Once again, this is a demonstration of the critical nature of relationships. If the discipler had taken a hard-line approach to sharing the good news by some evangelistic method, the results may have looked completely different.

Figure 3.7
How long was it from the time Jesus first came up in conversation with this person until you gave your life to Him?

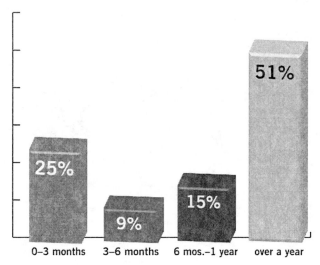

| 0–3 months | 3–6 months | 6 mos.–1 year | over a year |

Embedded deeply in the process of making disciples are the character traits of the discipler. As chapter two outlined, Jesus exhibited character traits that defined him and his ministry. Jesus demonstrated these characteristics so powerfully that Christianity is the largest religion in the world today. Did disciplers in this study have certain characteristics that were effective in guiding someone to follow Jesus? The answer is an emphatic yes. From a list of twenty characteristics and a fill-in-the-blank option, unbelievers designated the character traits that impacted their decision to become disciples of Jesus. There were seven character traits that were deemed as statistically significant to making disciples. Those character traits were love, faithfulness, authenticity, knowledge, trust, care, and passion (see figure 3.8). Nineteen percent of those who were unbelievers indicated that love had the biggest impact on their decision to follow Jesus. Faithfulness was the second highest with 13 percent, followed by authenticity with 8.5 percent, knowledge with 8.3 percent, trust with 7.4 percent, care with 7.2 percent, and—last but not least—passion, which was indicated by 6.8 percent of respondents. The remaining 29.3 percent of responses was comprised of character traits that were of lesser significance, and were not included.

Figure 3.8
Which one of this person's character traits had the biggest impact on your decision to give your life to Jesus?

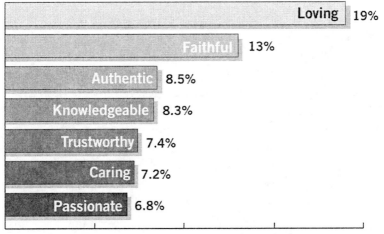

Loving	19%
Faithful	13%
Authentic	8.5%
Knowledgeable	8.3%
Trustworthy	7.4%
Caring	7.2%
Passionate	6.8%

The remaining 29.28% was comprised of traits that were of lesser significance.

At this point, it may be valuable to notice what characteristics were not significant to making disciples. From the list of characteristics provided and the fill-in-the-blank option, traits that did not significantly contribute to discipling others were: boldness, gentleness, humility, joy, patience, giving, forgiving, goodness, kindness, peacefulness, self-control, and courage. In fact, seven of these characteristics are listed as fruits of the Spirit in Galatians 5:22–23! Rounding out the bottom four least significant characteristics were (in no particular order): peacefulness, self-control, kindness, and courage. This is not to suggest that none of these traits are important in discipling others or in leading a life committed to God; however, it is crucial to know which characteristics have the most influence on others and which have little influence on them.

The data revealed in this chapter outline the characteristics crucial to intentional discipleship. It is illuminating to recognize that these are all traits that Jesus demonstrated. Once we begin to emulate Jesus in our lives, unbelievers will be drawn to the life-changing power of the gospel and respond to it.

SUMMARY OF INTENTIONAL DISCIPLERS

As the research revealed, most of the time, people become disciples of Jesus through a one-on-one relationship between an unbeliever and an intentional discipler. The gender of the discipler is more likely male than female (although there are some differences that will be pointed out in a later chapter). The most common age of the intentional discipler is between twenty-nine and forty-three years old, and most of the time, he is a relative (again, there are some exceptions). In the overwhelming majority of cases, intentional disciplers were the ones who initiated conversations about Jesus; and, in almost half of the cases, it took disciplers less than three months of knowing unbelievers before they instigated spiritual dialogue. The majority of the time, it took more than a year for intentional disciplers to lead someone to Jesus; and the character traits that had the biggest influence in persuading unbelievers to become disciples of Christ were love, faithfulness, authenticity, knowledge, trust, care, and passion.

Are any of these results surprising? Keep in mind that these findings are generalizations. More specific correlations will be made in subsequent chapters.

Does the profile of an intentional discipler correspond with what you portray to others? It is likely that you know someone who needs Jesus. What is holding you back from sharing the good news with him or her? Are you afraid to bring up Jesus in conversation with that person? Do you have the patience and commitment to disciple him or her for a long period of time? Do you exhibit love, authenticity, care, and passion? Are you faithful, trustworthy, and knowledgeable? These are some of the difficult questions you must raise if you desire to intentionally disciple others. Obedience to the Great Commission requires sensitive hearts, resilient minds, and a tough faith that can repel the discouraging arrows of Satan. It is a call to live dangerously.

The next several chapters are devoted to examining the character traits that influenced people to become disciples of Jesus. Correlations between these traits and other variables, such as relationships and genders, will be discussed. Each character trait will be examined in detail, with examples of how we can demonstrate those qualities to others. As each characteristic is discussed, ask yourself if you currently exhibit that trait, and how you can strengthen it in your life to influence others.

QUESTIONS FOR DISCUSSION

- Do you have any perceptions about the conversion process that have changed as a result of reading this chapter? What?

- The research revealed that, in the majority of cases, an unbeliever is led to Jesus through a one-on-one relationship with another person. What does this tell us about our relationships with unbelievers?

- Read Galatians 5:22–23. Which of these fruits are characteristics of influential disciplers? Which are not? Does this surprise you?

- Most of the time, disciplers are the ones who initiate spiritual discussions with unbelievers. What does this tell us about our role in discipling others?

- The majority of the time, it takes more than a year for an unbeliever to become a follower of Jesus. Why do you think this is so?

PERSONAL REFLECTION

- What is a characteristic that you can intentionally develop to help you be a more effective discipler?

- Ask God to mold your heart to give you the wisdom, faith, and fortitude to intentionally disciple others.

4

An Intentional Discipler Is Loving

To love someone means to see him as God intended him.

—FYODOR DOSTOEVSKY

LOVE IS THE FIRST key to intentional discipleship. According to people who were unbelievers, this is the character trait that had the biggest impact on their decision to follow Jesus. This should come as no surprise. Jesus demonstrated love to people everywhere he went. As a result, their lives were forever changed. Jesus lived dangerously because he was compelled to love people, and he did not let anyone or anything get in the way of expressing it. Love flowed out of him and touched the lives of those he met.

In his interactions with people, Jesus did things no contemporary leaders of his time dreamed of doing—he fearlessly accepted the downcasts of society. One such act of love is illustrated beautifully in the account of the woman caught in adultery. The Pharisees and teachers of the law brought the woman before Jesus. Notice the exchange between the Pharisees, Jesus, and the woman from John 8:5–11:

> In the Law Moses commanded us to stone such women. Now what do you say?" They were using this question as a trap, in order to have a basis for accusing him. But Jesus bent down and started to write on the ground with his finger. When they kept on questioning him, he straightened up and said to them, "If any one of you is without sin, let him be the first to throw a stone at her. Again he stooped down and wrote on the ground. At this, those who heard began to go away one at a time, the older ones first, until only Jesus was left, with the woman still standing there. Jesus straightened up and asked her, "Woman, where are they? Has no one condemned you?" "No one, sir," she said. "Then neither do I condemn you," Jesus declared. "Go now and leave your life of sin.

In this simple, yet poignant act of love, Jesus offered the woman protection, grace, and forgiveness, even though he knew the Pharisees and teachers were trying to ensnare him.

This story has implications for us today. Like the woman caught in adultery, there are many people in society who feel rejected or unwanted. To complicate this predicament, many people today have experienced suffering from the loss of a loved one, sustained abuse of some kind, or they have experienced the pain of failed relationships. There is no quick fix to these maladies, but the love of Jesus can heal many wounds. We, as Christ followers, are called to show them the restorative love of Jesus through our actions and attitudes.

Jesus did not come to enforce a list of rules or set of twisted religious beliefs like the Pharisees; he taught us something much simpler: how to love others. If the concept of love is truly absorbed and assimilated into the core of our being, it will radiate from us as we interact with unbelievers, and they will come to see a love that transcends religion. We are called to be beacons of love, and light the way to Jesus.

Unfortunately, disciples of Jesus sometimes prematurely criticize others without bothering to find out if there are extenuating circumstances. This has left countless people with a distrustful outlook toward Christianity. For example, there may be valid reasons why someone is homeless or poor. Jesus gave people the benefit of the doubt and intentionally sought to show them his love. When we follow the example of Jesus by loving unbelievers, they will be receptive to the gospel.

We have the capacity to love because Jesus first demonstrated his love for us. The apostle John said, "We love because he first loved us. If anyone says, 'I love God,' yet hates his brother, he is a liar. For anyone who does not love his brother, whom he has seen, cannot love God, whom he has not seen" (1 John 4:19–20). Would you go so far as to be like Jesus and protect someone who is considered to be a sinner? Loving others is dangerous! It involves a certain amount of risk. Loving others is not always easy, and we may be opening ourselves up to judgment from other disciples of Jesus. Do you have the capability to forgive someone who has wronged you personally? Jesus continued to love others even during his arrest. When Peter cut off the ear of the high priest's servant, Jesus reached out his hand and healed the man. Jesus loved at all times.

INFLUENCE OF LOVE ON DISCIPLES

Relationship plays a significant role in the influence of love on unbeliev-ers. All disciplers who displayed love influenced unbelievers to accept Jesus, but unbelievers were much more likely to be influenced by relatives than by any other type of relationship. As figure 4.1 illustrates, 77 percent of disciplers who influenced others to accept Jesus by demonstrating love were related to the unbelievers. Ten percent of disciplers who exhibited love were friends with the unbelievers, 9 percent were ministers, and the remaining 4 percent of disciplers included various other types of relation-ships. This underscores not only the importance of showing love to oth-ers, but points to the exceptional impact relatives have on unbelievers.

Figure 4.1
Influence of love based on relationship

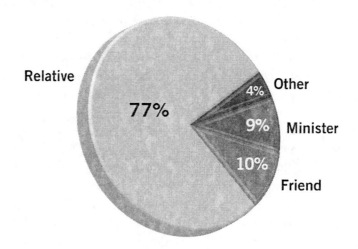

It is revealing to know that our relationships with relatives make us seven times more likely to have an influence on their lives than people who are not related to them. We can dismiss this correlation, or we can acknowledge it and pay special attention to our roles as potential disciplers.

Figure 4.2
Influence of love based on discipler's gender

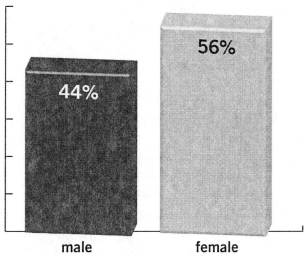

| male | female |

The gender of those who exhibit love to unbelievers is also notable. Figure 4.2 reveals that 56 percent of all disciplers who displayed love to unbelievers were women, while the remaining 44 percent of disciplers were men. This can imply at least two things: 1) women are more likely than men to influence unbelievers by exhibiting love, or 2) unbelievers perceive women as displaying love to a stronger extent than men. In either case, this revelation suggests that women may have a more natural inclination to express love to others, and men need to focus more of their energy on demonstrating love in their discipling relationships.

CHARACTERISTICS OF LOVING DISCIPLERS

What does it mean to demonstrate love to others? When unbelievers who were influenced by love were asked to give an example of how their disciplers exhibited love, three chief answers were given. According to unbelievers, people who displayed love to them were accepting, compassionate, and sacrificial.

A Loving Discipler Is Accepting

The first way we can demonstrate love to others is by accepting them. When I was working with a church a few years ago, an unbelieving couple who had been living together asked if they could get married in our church building. They had already made the same request of several other churches in town, but were flatly refused because they were required to become Christians first. We decided to let them use the building. The rationale was that—by accepting this couple—a seed would be planted, and they would eventually come to the Lord. That is exactly what happened. A few years later, the couple decided that their children needed to learn the Bible, and they started coming to church. This led to a discipling relationship with one of our members, which brought them to conversion. They remain faithful disciples of Jesus to this day! It all happened because our church demonstrated acceptance and love to them.

People are judged on everything from their skin color to their political beliefs. Being nonjudgmental can be problematic for disciples of Jesus. When we tout messages on bumper stickers such as, "Not perfect, just forgiven," we are conveying a certain smugness that repels unbelievers. A common cry among unbelievers is that Christians are intolerant and narrow-minded. If we want others to feel comfortable around us, we need to break the stereotype and accept them.

Many unbelievers indicated that acceptance was a crucial ingredient that led them to Jesus. Tracy* summed up the sentiments of many when she said of her discipler, "She dealt with my questions and insecurities without judging me or telling me what I should do . . . she loved me in everything I did, whether she approved of it or not." Susan agreed. "It doesn't matter if I mess up or if I don't understand something, he's still going to love me. In a way, that's shown me how God can love me even when everything is still wrong."

Accepting others unconditionally is a common theme in discipleship. Jesus demonstrated love by initiating relationships with prostitutes, tax collectors, and "sinners." We are often reluctant to associate with certain kinds of people, because we do not know how to handle the sin in their lives or we are afraid that others may judge us for having relationships with them. When we let fear control us, we miss out on many opportunities to make disciples. Accepting others is dangerous, because it demands

* Names are changed to protect anonymity.

that we get rid of our personal biases. It may be that God is deliberately planning for us to disciple someone we would not ordinarily consider.

All people have sin in their lives. The problem is that some sins are more obvious than others. The unwed pregnant teenager cannot hide her sin, but the preacher addicted to Internet porn is just as guilty. Jesus loved everyone regardless of their sin; it was his modus operandi. Like Jesus, we are called to accept others without reservation. This does not mean we should accept sin; it means engaging in a loving relationship with someone who is struggling with sin. Making disciples is a process of teaching someone what it means to be in a relationship with Jesus. When this happens, they will recognize and respond to the voice of Jesus, "Go now and leave your life of sin."

It is often easier for us to ignore people until they get their lives straightened out. But this is dead wrong! Judging others will send them far from the accepting arms of Jesus. Just as Jesus accepts sinners, we need to accept unbelievers for who they are—children of God. This is not to say we should dismiss sin. Through the process of making disciples, we will ultimately guide unbelievers to repent of their sin. Adopting the nonjudgmental attitude of Jesus provides unbelievers with a needed respite from the harsh criticisms of the world.

When we love people who are considered undesirable, they are open to the gospel. Jennifer said, "He loved me when I felt unloved. He became the only light in my life when I was only around things that were dark." Can you sense Jennifer's gratitude? She felt despised and reviled by others, but the love of Jesus enveloped her and brought her into relationship with him. Jesus warms the hearts of those who are broken, lonely, and depressed.

Intentional discipleship begins with accepting others. If we do not have the capacity to accept unbelievers unconditionally, it is time to take deliberate steps to change ourselves into more loving disciples of Jesus. When we accept unbelievers, they will understand the hope that Jesus offers and respond to the good news.

A Loving Discipler Is Compassionate

Love is also demonstrated to unbelievers when we express compassionate attitudes. Jesus was compassionate; he continually sought to encourage and bless others with his presence. When Jesus was on the cross, the words he spoke were overflowing with compassion. In Luke 23:34, Jesus said,

"Father, forgive them, for they do not know what they are doing." When one of the criminals asked Jesus to remember him, Jesus assured the man, in Luke 23:43, "I tell you the truth, today you will be with me in paradise." As Jesus looked down from the cross and saw his mother and John, he pleaded, in John 19:26–27, "Dear woman, here is your son," and to the disciple, "Here is your mother." Even during his most trying time, Jesus remained dedicated to loving others because he was compassionate.

Disciplers influence unbelievers by demonstrating compassion to them. Rather than becoming deeply involved in someone's life, it is much easier to keep a safe distance from that person. However, unbelievers indicated that this approach does not work. Amy's discipler was faithful. "He was always there for me no matter the situation," she said. Similarly, John said, "He was there for me every time I messed up." Unbelievers appreciate disciplers who are physically and emotionally present.

A compassionate discipler was also viewed as someone who encourages others. Martha indicated that her discipler demonstrated love through encouragement. She said, "He always noticed me and encouraged me." "I observed hugs and real concern when he talked to others."

Corey agreed. "She just really cared for and loved me. I was making a lot of mistakes in my life, and she was the one person who saw the good in me and knew that I was better than what I had become. She has always loved and cared for me." Encouragement can take many forms—verbal support, physical assurance, or positive reinforcement. Part of making disciples is encouraging and showing our support to others through their struggles.

Making disciples is not an easy task; it taxes our resources and our emotions. It is an endeavor that requires us to forfeit our selfish desires for the sake of others. This may mean training ourselves to encourage others; it may involve relinquishing our pet peeves. Above all, it means being like Jesus by committing ourselves to thinking about the needs of others.

A Loving Discipler Is Sacrificial

Disciplers also demonstrate love by having a sacrificial attitude. Being sacrificial requires us to take our focus off of pleasing ourselves. This has caused many unnecessary disagreements in churches. We insist on worshipping a certain way, we complain if sermons are too long, if the heat or air-conditioning is not to our standards, or what clothes are appropriate to wear in the sanctuary. It is quite natural to get caught up in these superficial matters when we are more concerned about ourselves than others. If we are sacrificially concerned with the welfare of others, such differences become inconsequential. To make things worse, when unbelievers come into our churches and see us bickering over trivial matters—and they *are* trivial to unbelievers—we can be assured they will quickly sprint toward the doors. Jesus said, in John 13:35, "By this all men will know that you are my disciples, if you love one another." Who wants to be part of a church that is full of squabbling people who cannot get along with each other? Unbelievers experience too much abuse in the world as it is! We need to show them that being a disciple of Jesus means leading a noble, joyful life.

Jesus loved us so much that he gave his very life for us. Can you think of a more supreme act of sacrifice? Jesus did not have to die; he could have called thousands of angels to rescue him. He did not. In the single greatest act of love ever, Jesus chose to put himself through humiliation, beatings, pain, and suffering because it enabled our sins to be forgiven forever. His example of giving spread like wildfire from one person to another for two thousand years.

We do not have to die for others like Jesus did for us, but we can certainly learn from the example he set for us. We can be intentional disciplers by giving our energy and efforts to lead others to the cross of Jesus. According to Trevor, his discipler "Always cared and was very giving; he put everyone else first." Jenny echoed this sentiment. "He always put himself last, and he had a do-unto-others type of attitude." These statements indicate that love is shown through an attitude of giving—not through the giving of gifts—but through an attitude of sacrificial love.

Being a disciple of Jesus is a happy life, but it is not a lazy life. Some take a minimalist approach to love by serving in a soup kitchen or volunteering at a hospital once a month. These acts are done out of a good conscience and they meet needs, but they do not achieve long-lasting results. We need to take it to the next level and make a permanent difference in the spiritual lives of others. Serving others requires many of us to seismically shift our thinking. Discipleship requires lifelong devotion through a servant attitude of meekness. It is not about what is best for us, but what is beneficial to others. This is accomplished by spending time modeling Jesus, teaching, and guiding others down the path of following Jesus. It is a process that turns our contented world on end by propelling us into sacrificial relationships with others.

Demonstrating love can perhaps be best summarized by Erin's experience, who aptly described her discipler this way: "This man treated people like Jesus treated them: Like men and women created in the image of God, with different strengths, different weaknesses, different gifts; like the sons and daughters God wants us all so desperately to become. Whether speaking to a congregation or chatting on a lakeside, this man treated people humbly, honestly, and lovingly, with grace and truth."

It is fascinating to notice how much intentional disciplers loved unbelievers. We need to learn from their examples, and strive to lead lives that demonstrate love to them. Our mandate is to love one another by being sacrificial.

LOVE FOSTERS SPIRITUAL DISCUSSIONS

One of the biggest obstacles we need to overcome in making disciples is their resistance to spiritual discussions. Unbelievers who were led to Jesus through a discipling relationship were asked, "Why did you feel comfortable discussing spiritual matters with this person?"

Unbelievers are comfortable engaging in spiritual matters with someone who is nonjudgmental. Betsy said of her discipler, "She was very loving and accepting of where I was in my walk with God, and didn't judge my past. Instead, she lovingly addressed my concerns and lifestyle as a sister or best friend would, and didn't condemn me. I felt comfortable opening up to her." Brett agreed. "We had a close relationship, and could talk about anything. He was someone I felt I could share anything with without being judged."

When we demonstrate love and acceptance to unbelievers instead of judgment, they will be compelled to share their hearts with us. "He created a nonjudgmental atmosphere in which I could openly express my heart," said Ingrid. "He loved me extravagantly." Treating others in a nonjudgmental manner encourages them to feel comfortable sharing their inner struggles with us, thus advancing the discipling relationship.

Having spiritual discussions with unbelievers is most effective when it is characterized by an attitude of grace. In Colossians 4:5–6, Paul said, "Be wise in the way you act toward outsiders; make the most of every opportunity. Let your conversation be always full of grace, seasoned with salt, so that you may know how to answer everyone." In Jesus' day, salt was a precious commodity. It added flavor to food and worked as a preservative. In the same way, Paul is admonishing us to flavor our conversations with unbelievers by seasoning them with words that build up others. If we judge them, we will see them slip through God's fingers. A gracious spirit will encourage disciples to take hold of God's loving hands. Being like salt also means we can act as agents to preserve God's Word by sharing the gospel with others.

If we have nonjudgmental attitudes or our biases prevent us from engaging in dialogue with people who are gay, pro-choice, or homeless, we are not prepared for a life of disciple making. We need to look to the example of Jesus, and allow him to teach us acceptance, compassion, and humility. For those of us who are able to accept others despite our differences, we are on the road to becoming intentional disciplers.

THE CHALLENGE OF LOVING OTHERS

Are you a loving person? Most people would make that claim. The challenge is putting your beliefs into practice. Many unbelievers will not automatically assume that you have love in your heart unless you show them. To them, a Christian is no better than anyone else. It is up to you to demonstrate to them the love that Jesus has revealed to you. If you desire to disciple others, you must intentionally love them as Jesus loved his disciples. It also means getting rid of any biases that can easily get in the way of showing love. Loving others is easy when you accept people who look like you and think like you. Loving others means accepting them unconditionally, despite potential consequences you may face.

Loving others also means having a compassionate attitude. You cannot hold onto an agenda of fulfilling your needs and desires. You may run into situations that demand you to take action based on kindness or empathy. If you cannot respond in this manner, you will not be an effective discipler. Being selfless means doing what you can to support and encourage unbelievers verbally and physically.

Additionally, making disciples involves leading a sacrificial life—one that is totally committed to the other person. Can you lay down your life for your friends and family, as well as for unbelievers? Consider the actions of Jesus and think about the potential influence you can have on unbelievers by placing them first.

Are you willing to demonstrate love in these ways? If not, it is time to work on becoming more spiritually loving. If you are ready and equipped for the challenge, then get to work! Making disciples is an incredible and rewarding ride for you and for unbelievers!

QUESTIONS FOR DISCUSSION

- Who was the most loving person you remember as a child? How did he or she demonstrate love to you?

- If you were the woman caught in adultery (John 8:5–11), how would you have responded to Jesus' admonishment to, "Go now and leave your life of sin"?

- What personal biases do you possess that may get in the way of accepting others unconditionally?

- Why do you think people are influenced to become disciples by someone who encourages them? What can you do to encourage others?

- Read Colossians 4:5–6. What specific things can you do to ensure that your conversations with unbelievers are "seasoned with salt"?

PERSONAL REFLECTION

- What are some ways you can serve your friends and family, as well as unbelievers?

- Ask God to guide you to become a potential influence on unbelievers by loving them.

5

An Intentional Discipler Is Faithful

God will never, never, never let us down if we have faith and put our trust in Him. He will always look after us. So we must cleave to Jesus. Our whole life must simply be woven into Jesus.

—MOTHER TERESA

THE SECOND KEY TO intentional discipleship is faithfulness. Jesus was an intentional discipler because he was faithful to God, his followers, and to the Scriptures. He remained resolutely faithful in the face of opposition. His example of faithfulness impacted the lives of unbelievers and transformed them into his disciples.

The finest example of Jesus' faithfulness was demonstrated by his willingness to die on the cross. This was evidenced through the attitude he expressed before and during his crucifixion. Notice the unwavering faithfulness of Jesus in the garden of Gethsemane:

> They went to a place called Gethsemane, and Jesus said to his disciples, "Sit here while I pray." He took Peter, James and John along with him, and he began to be deeply distressed and troubled. "My soul is overwhelmed with sorrow to the point of death," he said to them. "Stay here and keep watch." Going a little farther, he fell to the ground and prayed that if possible the hour might pass from him. "Abba, Father," he said, "everything is possible for you. Take this cup from me. Yet not what I will, but what you will." Then he returned to his disciples and found them sleeping. "Simon," he said to Peter, "are you asleep? Could you not keep watch for one hour?" (Mark 14:32–37).

There are several observations we can draw from this narrative. First, Jesus begged God to free him from his impending crucifixion; yet in his very next breath, Jesus completely surrendered his will to God.

49

Unquestionably, he did not wish to die, but Jesus never doubted his faithfulness to God, his disciples, and all future generations.

Further, in the middle of his anguish, Jesus remained faithful in his relationship with God. He was able to approach the throne of God in prayer because of his great faithfulness. This was not easy for Jesus; his distress was so great that Luke asserted, in Luke 22:44, "his sweat was like drops of blood falling to the ground." The knowledge of his looming crucifixion would have crushed the spirit of a less faithful person. Nevertheless, Jesus was able to bow in obedience to God because of his abiding faithfulness and determined resolve.

Another observation we can make about Jesus in Gethsemane is that he remained faithful in prayer, despite the lack of support from his closest disciples. Jesus asked them to keep watch, but when he returned after an hour of prayer, he found his disciples fast asleep. His faithfulness unfazed, Jesus continued praying. This happened three times before the crowd came to arrest Jesus. Knowing that his disciples were sleeping, Jesus could easily have lost the desire and strength to continue praying—yet he remained faithful.

We can learn from Jesus' example of faithfulness. He was firmly devoted to God, even when his own life was at stake. Likewise, we need to be faithful to God, even if it conflicts with our own desires. The dilemma of remaining faithful occurs when God's principles, circumstances, or timing get in the way of our own self-interests. It is then that our faith is tested and refined. If we choose to continue in a relationship with God through our trials, we will recognize his presence, and our faith will grow by leaps and bounds.

Making disciples is accomplished by having a faith that is revealed through our interactions with unbelievers. The apostle Paul challenged the saints at Philippi to "shine like stars" in a dark world (Phil 2:15). The faith we have in Jesus will light the way for others who are going through personal struggles. This requires us to be open to unbelievers about difficulties we have experienced. They need to see that—although we are not perfect—we can relate to their struggles and doubts. When they understand that our own faith in God has helped us overcome personal temptations and influences, they will see Jesus living in us.

Faithfulness is having a relationship with Jesus that is so powerful and so tangled with our souls that it is expressed naturally in our relationships with others. Being faithful is not something we do; it is who we are. If we are not fully dedicated to God, we need to emulate the faithfulness of Jesus.

INFLUENCE OF FAITHFULNESS ON DISCIPLES

Disciplers who demonstrate faithfulness influence unbelievers to commit their lives to Jesus. The research revealed that unbelievers were much more likely to be influenced by relatives who demonstrated faithfulness than by any other type of relationship. As figure 5.1 indicates, 65 percent of all disciplers who exhibited faithfulness were related to unbelievers; 15 percent of disciplers were ministers, and 13 percent of those who had influential faith were friends of unbelievers. The remaining 7 percent was comprised of other relationships. The faithfulness of relatives had more impact on unbelievers than all other relationships combined. This was expected, since just over half of all disciplers who influenced unbelievers to follow Jesus were related to them. However, this does not account for the increased percentage gap between relatives and all other relationships when faithfulness was identified as an influential factor in making disciples. Clearly, relatives were considered to be influential because they exhibited faithfulness more than any other type of relationship.

Figure 5.1
Influence of faithfulness based on relationship

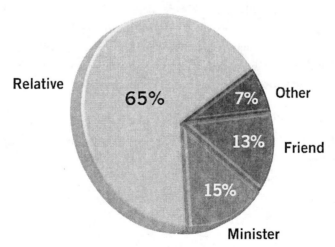

Knowing that relatives have such a great influence on unbelievers by displaying faithfulness challenges us to be more aware of our own influences on others. If we are related to someone who is not a disciple of Jesus, we need to recognize the incredible influence we potentially have by demonstrating our faithfulness to him. If we are not related to an unbeliever, we are not excused from the challenge to share our faith.

CHARACTERISTICS OF FAITHFUL DISCIPLERS

Being faithful is somewhat of an enigma. How can faithfulness be quantified? We may be faithful, but to what or to whom? The study shed some light on these questions. Disciples who were influenced by faithfulness were asked to give an example of how their disciplers were faithful. The results revealed that a faithful discipler was submissive to God, remained obedient to him, and had a mature faith.

A Faithful Discipler Is Submissive

One aspect of demonstrating faithfulness to unbelievers is by being submissive to God's will. Many former unbelievers indicated that their disciplers expressed submission to God by remaining faithful to him during difficult times. "When faced with life-threatening challenges, he held firm to his beliefs and to his faith in Christ," said Robert. Similarly, Donna relayed that her discipler was submissive. "He remained faithful through his parents' divorce, he had skin cancer, and he had an aneurysm and stroke. Still, he praises the Lord." These people were touched spiritually by disciples of Jesus who remained faithful to God despite difficult obstacles in their own lives. Disciplers impacted unbelievers by sharing how they remained submissive to God in the face of adversity. This example of submission influenced unbelievers to ultimately follow Jesus. Ordinary Christians resign their faith and blame God for their troubles, but faithful disciplers choose to be like Jesus and display extraordinary faith during trying times.

Unbelievers are always watching followers of Jesus. Some anticipate the worst; others have little or no expectations. All of them are curious to see how we will handle difficulties—if we will remain faithful or if we will give up on God and walk away from him.

I have an agnostic friend who has seen his Christian friends experience many struggles. He told me he is always struck by their steadfast faithfulness to God. As far as I know, he still has not given his life to Jesus, but the seed of faithfulness has been planted in him. When he eventually faces trials in his own life, he may remember the example of his Christians friends and look to God for strength. This is the kind of faith that will spur others to know Jesus!

Demonstrating faithfulness shows unbelievers that we depend upon God's strength. Paul said in Philippians 4:13, "I can do everything through him who gives me strength." It is hard to imagine enduring difficulties without the strength that Jesus so freely gives! When we depend on God's strength to carry us through our trials, it influences unbelievers to follow Jesus. June said, "She remained faithful to God even when she was going through hard times—she was diagnosed with cancer, and still held on to God."

Our faithfulness will also inspire unbelievers to tap into the healing power that God provides. Phil summed up this process when he said, "I have watched this person for years, and he has provided nothing but a positive example for me. Bad things have happened, good things have happened, and still this person remains faithful to God."

Although our ultimate goal is guiding unbelievers to be shaped into the image of Jesus, they will first learn from our actions and will emulate our habits—both positive and negative. If we remain faithful to God in trying times, they will understand that we lean upon his sovereign power, and our example will influence them to do the same.

A Faithful Discipler Is Obedient

Another way we can demonstrate faithfulness to unbelievers is by remaining obedient to God. In an age of moral relativism, obedience to anyone or anything is often frowned upon. Nevertheless, unbelievers noted that influential disciplers exhibited obedience to God. Donna said, "She did whatever the Lord asked of her, to the best of her abilities, and had tremendous faith that he would provide for her."

Although Jesus fervently prayed that he would not have to endure a cruel and painful death, he chose to be obedient to God. Obeying God is not always pleasant or easy; it demands a faithful heart that is committed to serving him. Disciplers who demonstrate obedience to God influence unbelievers to follow him. Jackson said, "He did his best to follow God wherever he was led."

Knowing God's will for our lives is sometimes difficult to discern. It may require us to take a step of faith. My hometown is built around the Chena River. When the river freezes in the winter, it forms an "ice bridge" that provides a shortcut from one side of the river to the other. Every winter, we wait until the ice is several feet thick before attempting to drive over the frozen river. Still, the first time we drive off the road and down the riverbank, we can feel our adrenaline pumping through our veins. There is always a little fear that the ice will crack under the weight of our vehicle and we will end up at the bottom of the river. Remaining obedient to God is sometimes like driving off a road and onto an ice bridge. We are not always sure if he will hold our weight or let us drown.

When we are obedient to God, unbelievers take notice of our faithfulness and follow suit. Kelly said, "He did what he believed Christ wanted him to do." As disciplers, our mandate is to demonstrate faithfulness by being obedient to God.

A Faithful Discipler Is Mature

Intentional disciplers are also mature in their faith. Having a mature faith has a positive influence on unbelievers. Faith is a dynamic, growing process. It does not naturally develop with age. There are many young disciples of Jesus who have a strong faith, just as there are older Christians who have a relatively weak faith. Faithfulness is a transformational process. It takes time, effort, and work.

Unbelievers indicated two disciplines that contributed to the mature faith of their disciplers: prayer and attention to God's Word. Don said, "This person was committed to regular, habitual prayer." Sarah simply said, "He is a prayer warrior."

How does prayer demonstrate mature faith to an unbeliever? When we pray with—and for—an unbeliever, the power of prayer is made apparent to them. Prayer also trains unbelievers to understand that we pray in anticipation of God's intervention in our lives. Praying with them further demonstrates our humility in bowing before the Master of the universe. We want to teach them that the man who can kneel before God can stand before anyone else.

When unbelievers see us live out our faithfulness through an active prayer life, they will begin to understand the power of having absolute reliance on God. We need to share our prayers with others as we disciple them. When we pray with them and for them, they will be able to see an active, vibrant faith. As we pray with them, it is crucial to keep track of the many ways God has answered prayers. Then they can develop an appreciation for the power of prayer. Prayer provides opportunities to develop faithfulness.

The Word of God was also highlighted by several unbelievers as an indication of the mature faithfulness of disciplers. "No matter what happened, he was always, continuously in God's Word," said Sam. Tara observed that her discipler also paid attention to Scripture. "She always measured every decision through Scripture." Jesus fed himself spiritually from the Word of God, and he discipled others to do the same. Likewise, when we spend time in the Scriptures, we are not only helping our faith mature, but are also increasing the faith of unbelievers.

Growing and developing our faith is a lifelong process. It takes focused effort and consistent exercise through prayer and Bible study. When I was on the swim team in high school, we practiced for several hours Monday through Friday. We took Saturday and Sunday off. After resting on the weekends, practices on Mondays were always more difficult because of the interruption in training. Spiritual training is similar to physical training—it takes continuous, rigorous effort, and our spiritual lives suffer if we are not consistent in our discipline. In 1 Timothy 4:8 NLT, Paul told Timothy, "Physical training is good, but training for godliness is much better, promising benefits in this life and in the life to come."

Being an intentional discipler means taking the responsibility to continually grow and develop our faith. We need to be strong enough to withstand the questions, pressures, and deep responsibility that discipling thrusts upon us. Although we should strive to have a mature faith, we should never reach the point where we think we have spiritually "arrived." We cannot achieve spiritual maturity if we are arrogant. We need to take an honest assessment of our faith. If it is not up to snuff, we need to purposely strengthen it through a diet of prayer and Bible study; then, we need to share our growth experiences with others. Spiritual food sustains us and nourishes our growth into the image of Jesus.

THE CHALLENGE OF BEING FAITHFUL

Do you have a strong faith? If you are struggling in your faith, you have no business discipling others. Conversely, if you have experienced difficulties in your life and your faith has grown stronger as a result, your story will have a huge impact on your disciples. Is your faith strong enough to share with others? Is it vibrant and active, or is it at risk of becoming stale and tepid? Do others see you caught up in a committed and reverent prayer life? Do they know that you are reading your Bible faithfully and growing from its message? Do they observe you being submissive to God by trusting him with your struggles, or do they see someone who depends on his own faculties?

If your faith is not strong, your relationships with unbelievers may spiritually weaken you. Discipling others calls you to rise above mediocre faith—it demands you to be prepared to fight off negative pressures and temptations. Jesus charges you to live dangerously with your life by never letting your faith become idle or stagnant.

If you were standing next to a huge chasm and God told you to jump into the void, would you do it? God is asking you to surrender to his will. This is not an easy task. Being faithful to God takes work. There is no easy way out. It takes time and effort to strengthen your faith. It takes courage, fortitude and grit. Before you can intentionally disciple others, God wants to be assured that you can take the leap of faith to seek his wisdom and trust his guidance in your life.

QUESTIONS FOR DISCUSSION

- Think about a person who was instrumental in your spiritual development. Describe how this person was faithful.

- What trials have you been through that you have overcome by being submissive to God?

- Read Philippians 4:13. How is this verse assuring to you? How can it encourage unbelievers?

- How would you rate your faith on a scale of 1 to 10, with 1 being the weakest and 10 being the strongest? Explain.

- Read 1 Timothy 4:8. What is one area of your spiritual life that could be strengthened through training?

PERSONAL REFLECTION

- What things in your life are you willing to relegate to second place to give you more time with unbelievers?

- Make a commitment to increase your prayer time with God this week. For example, if you are currently spending ten minutes a day in prayer, increase it to twenty minutes.

6

An Intentional Discipler Is Authentic

A real Christian is a person who can give his pet parrot
to the town gossip.

—BILLY GRAHAM

THE THIRD KEY TO intentional discipleship is authenticity. The authentic nature of Jesus contributed to his effectiveness as a discipler. Even his enemies knew that Jesus would never misrepresent himself. After he had been arrested, mocked and beaten, Jesus was brought before the council leaders and elders. Luke records the conversation that transpired: "If you are the Christ," they said, "tell us." Jesus answered, "If I tell you, you will not believe me, and if I asked you, you would not answer. But from now on, the Son of Man will be seated at the right hand of the mighty God." They all asked, "Are you then the Son of God?" He replied, "You are right in saying I am" (Luke 22:67–70). Even in the face of death, Jesus remained shamelessly authentic. He lived dangerously!

There was also no pretense in Jesus' life. When he was sad, he wept; when he felt compassion for people, he healed them; and when he was angry with the Pharisees, he called them hypocrites, fools, and snakes. People who interacted with Jesus knew where they stood with him. A centurion asked Jesus to heal his paralyzed servant, and Jesus said in Matthew 8:10, "I tell you the truth, I have not found anyone in Israel with such great faith." Peter told Jesus that he would never be killed, and Jesus cried out, "Get behind me, Satan!" (Matt 16:23). Jesus called it as he saw it because he was authentic. People may have disagreed with Jesus' message or methods, but they certainly could not criticize him for misrepresenting himself.

Too often, unbelievers expect the worst from disciples of Jesus. They watch us—waiting for us to mess up—so they can say, "See, I knew

Christians were all fakes." We have often advanced the notion among un-believers that we are insincere and disingenuous. Unbelievers have told me that they do not go to church because it is full of hypocrites. I agree! Believers are no better than anyone else. We all have faults and shortcom-ings. We are in fellowship with other disciples of Jesus because we need support and encouragement from them. We worship as a team. We can no more follow Jesus in isolation than we can play a game of football by ourselves!

If we model our lives after Jesus by being authentic in every situa-tion, others will respect us—even if they disagree with us. Our authentic lifestyle will encourage others to be like us and follow Jesus.

INFLUENCE OF AUTHENTICITY ON DISCIPLES

Unbelievers are influenced to commit their lives to Jesus by disciplers who exhibit authenticity in their lives. The research revealed that both men and women were influenced by the authenticity of disciplers, but men were influenced by authenticity to a higher degree than women. When relatives were filtered out of the data, male unbelievers were influenced by authenticity more than any other trait! Figure 6.1 shows that authenticity played the biggest role in influencing men, followed by passion, love, care, faithfulness, trust, and knowledge. Is this surprising? Before any explana-tions are suggested, it may be helpful to examine which gender is more likely to exhibit authenticity.

Figure 6.1
Characteristics that had the biggest influence on men
(filtered without relatives)

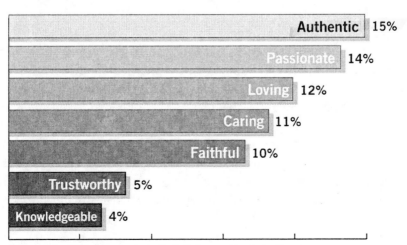

Authentic	15%
Passionate	14%
Loving	12%
Caring	11%
Faithful	10%
Trustworthy	5%
Knowledgeable	4%

The remaining 29% was comprised of traits that were of lesser significance.

According to the research, male disciplers demonstrated authenticity far more than female disciplers. Figure 6.2 shows that 74 percent of disciplers considered to be authentic were men, while only 26 percent were women—a ratio of almost three to one!

Figure 6.2
Influence of authenticity based on discipler's gender

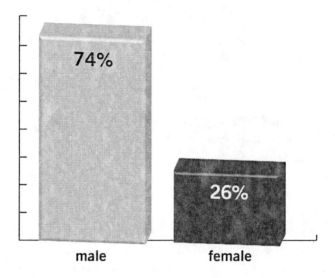

Not only are men more influenced than women by authenticity, they are also the ones who display this trait in their lives more often. Why is this? There may be many possible explanations. The data may reflect the different needs of men and women. Just as female disciplers naturally expressed love to a higher degree than male disciplers, authenticity may be expressed more strongly by men because of their innate differences. This could be interpreted to mean that women have a deeper need for love, and therefore naturally demonstrate this trait more strongly than men. Similarly, we can infer that men exhibit authenticity and are influenced by the trait more than women because they have a stronger need for authenticity in their lives.

Whatever the reasons, it is critical to know how unbelievers are influenced according to their gender. Male disciplers need to be aware of their natural tendencies to express authenticity in discipling others, and how it especially influences other men. For women disciplers, it is vital that their abilities to demonstrate love to others is not hindered; but rather, is freely expressed.

CHARACTERISTICS OF AUTHENTIC DISCIPLERS

If we come across as conceited or hypocritical, others will be repulsed by Christianity. Unbelievers who were influenced by authenticity were asked to give an example of how their disciplers were authentic. The results revealed that authentic disciplers were genuine in their interactions, transparent with their struggles, and consistent in their lifestyles.

An Authentic Discipler Is Genuine

Unbelievers are influenced by people who are genuine in their interactions with others. When I was a student at a Christian college, there were students who would sleep in on Sunday mornings and miss church. Once in a while, I noticed that one particular student would dress up in a suit and tie and go to the cafeteria to make it seem as if he attended services that morning. He probably never stopped to think about the negative example he was portraying to me or others.

If we only act as if we have genuine faith—but are insincere in our interactions with others—it will certainly backfire on us. Hypocritical actions repel unbelievers, but sincere relationships ultimately lead them to Jesus. Laurie said, "She was not afraid to be herself in every way. She was okay with not being good enough, with needing a Savior and having problems. She wasn't a hypocrite, and she wasn't pretending. She was a witness to the gospel just by being who she is, striving to do God's will." What a testimony of genuine faith! This discipler was a fallible person in every sense, yet she desired to honor God by being genuine. This authenticity is precisely what influenced Laurie and many others to give their lives to Jesus.

During his ministry, Jesus had many encounters with the Pharisees and teachers of the law. With each encounter, Jesus became increasingly frustrated with their lack of authenticity. Finally—when he could no longer take it—he gave them an earful. He told the crowds gathering around to listen to the teachings of the Pharisees, but warned them, "But do not do what they do, for they do not practice what they preach" (Matt 23:3). Jesus then unleashed a dangerous tirade aimed at exposing the Pharisees' problem: they were hypocrites. Listen to Jesus as he reprimands them in Matthew 23:23–28:

> "Woe to you, teachers of the law and Pharisees, you hypocrites! You give a tenth of your spices—mint, dill and cummin. But you have neglected the more important matters of the law—justice, mercy and faithfulness. You should have practiced the latter, without neglecting the former. You blind guides! You strain out a gnat but swallow a camel. Woe to you, teachers of the law and Pharisees, you hypocrites! You clean the outside of the cup and dish, but inside they are full of greed and self-indulgence. Blind Pharisee! First clean the inside of the cup and dish, and then the outside also will be clean. Woe to you, teachers of the law and Pharisees, you hypocrites! You are like whitewashed tombs, which look beautiful on the outside but on the inside are full of dead men's bones and everything unclean. In the same way, on the outside you appear to people as righteous but on the inside you are full of hypocrisy and wickedness."

To most people, the Pharisees appeared as models of authenticity, but they had abandoned one of the fundamental admonitions of the prophets—treat your fellow man with love and mercy. Jesus was telling them that they appeared clean and white on the outside, but on the inside they were rotting away from the filth of insincerity, pretense, and deceit.

Too often, Christians are seen as hypocritical, not authentic. The truth is that almost everyone—Christian or not—is inconsistent to some degree. It is our job to correct the perception that disciples of Jesus are hypocrites by paying special attention to being authentic—to have our insides match our outsides. Andrea summed up this idea when she said, "Unlike most so-called Christians we see around us, this guy was r-e-a-l."

Unbelievers can sense insincerity a mile away. If we do not exhibit authenticity, they will not trust us enough to open their hearts to us; but genuine relationships encourage unbelievers to know the Savior who offers sincere love. Sincerity emanates from us naturally as a result of following God and letting him take control of our entire lives.

An Authentic Discipler Is Transparent

Unbelievers also indicated that their disciplers demonstrated authenticity by being transparent with their struggles. When I was a teenager, I heard a speaker at a youth rally say, "I've never smoked; I've never had the urge to drink; I've never experimented with drugs, and I'm proud that I did the right thing." My friends and I all wondered, "This guy is unreal. What's the use in even trying?" Later, another speaker got up to speak whose message was very different. He said, "I used to smoke weed; I used to get drunk; I used to curse—but the grace of Jesus took away my urges and made me whole." This was a message we could all understand. I decided right then and there to be like the second speaker by being transparent with others.

Being transparent with others requires us to let down our guard. It also opens our hearts to others. When we express our own spiritual difficulties with unbelievers instead of acting like we are perfect, they will learn to emulate our genuineness, our humility, and our hope in God. Jeremy said, "He didn't hide his struggles, and I felt that he didn't put on a front like some people do about faith in Jesus Christ." Carrie echoed this sentiment. "This person was authentic as she told me about her struggles with anorexia as a young Christian, and how she finally trusted God and made her way out of that destructive lifestyle."

Additionally, our witness needs to speak from personal experience. When disciplers share their own struggles, it helps unbelievers understand that difficulties and suffering are part of the human condition. That is, everyone struggles, and no one is better than anyone else. The apostle Paul said in Romans 3:23: "for all have sinned and fall short of the glory of God." No one is perfect, but this is not the end of the story. Paul continues: "and are justified freely by his grace through the redemption that came by Christ Jesus (Rom 3:24).

People need to know what God has personally done for us—how his love has affected us, how he has been involved in our decision-making, and how he has given us hope. These are exciting revelations to share with others because we have the opportunity to reveal the joy that God has given us. When we share how God has worked in our lives, others will catch a glimpse of how they can benefit from being in relationship with him.

It is human nature to put up a false front. We want to appear tough and in control of our lives, even when the whole world may be crumbling around us. Jeff said, "He was transparent in sharing his life. He was never afraid to admit mistakes . . . and he spoke honestly about his own doubts and fears." A common misconception is that disciplers should never expose their faults to people they are guiding. The fear is that they will be perceived as weak and unable to lead effectively. This is patently untrue. A person who is transparent is viewed as having credibility.

The discipling relationship can be tricky. In some ways, disciplers are viewed by unbelievers as being superior—as having it all together. If we perpetuate this fallacy by presenting ourselves as faultless, when unbelievers discover that we have flaws we may lose their respect and our influence will be minimized, if not totally lost. The ultimate goal in modeling Jesus should be to guide unbelievers to Jesus—not to us. Being transparent will open the doors for this to happen.

Making disciples is not an employer/employee relationship. No one is the boss. It involves sharing our lives intimately with others. Can we adequately describe our journey in the faith with others? We need to be honest with our own sins, and communicate how God has brought us through our heartaches, struggles, and pain.

An Authentic Discipler Is Consistent

Authentic disciplers are also ones who demonstrate consistent lives to others. I live in the state of Oregon, which is considered to be one of the top three unchurched states in America. Developing relationships with unbelievers in Oregon requires an authentic expression of our faith to others and a consistency of actions. Being consistent is an enormous burden to bear. There are no simple steps to sharing the good news of Jesus. It involves much more than providing quality church programs, offering free Christian rock shows, or handing out church flyers. It means being intentionally authentic in our interactions with others. We do not have to be perfect; the key is being consistent in our behavior. We need to be the kind of example that others will follow to Jesus.

The writer of Hebrews said, in Hebrews 13:8, "Jesus Christ is the same yesterday, today and forever." Jesus never changes; he consistently loved his disciples and he continues that relationship with us today. Likewise, we need to lead lives that demonstrate consistency. If we do not have dependable behavior, we cannot effectively lead others. When times get tough for disciples, we need to be there to show them the healing hand of Jesus.

A consistent discipler influenced Beth. She said, "I knew it was the 'real deal' with her because I saw her actions match her words." In the same vein, Marty said, "He truly lived his faith. There were no discrepancies between what he said and how he acted."

A discipler who leads a consistent lifestyle is crucial to the faith development of an unbeliever. Leading others to Jesus is a tough job, but it becomes much more difficult if the discipler's behavior is unpredictable.

Until a disciple establishes a solid foundation of faith in Jesus Christ, disciplers are the ones who provide stability for them. We cannot say, "Do what I say, not what I do." If we display conflicting actions, it is easy for the disciple to get confused. However, if we are consistently faithful and disciples know what to expect from us, we will greatly influence others to know Jesus.

No one is perfect; we all sin. When we invariably blunder by sinning, our response will determine the level of influence we have on our disciples. If we ignore our sins or excuse them in any way, we will sabotage our discipling relationships. Others will assume we are hypocritical and will lack compassion when they sin. However, if we humbly acknowledge our weaknesses, ask for forgiveness, and strengthen our shortcomings, our authentic example will speak volumes to those we are discipling. Their fears will be alleviated and they will trust us to effectively disciple them.

AUTHENTICITY FOSTERS SPIRITUAL DISCUSSIONS

Unbelievers who were led to Jesus through a discipling relationship were asked, "Why did you feel comfortable discussing spiritual matters with this person?"

Unbelievers responded that they felt comfortable discussing spiritual matters with people who were authentic. Blake said, "I felt comfortable because he was a very understanding person. He cared about what was going on in my life and was willing to help me become a better person for God."

It takes a huge leap of confidence for an unbeliever to engage in spiritual conversations with someone. After all, talking about spiritual matters is a highly personal and potentially risky venture. Unbelievers instinctively know if we are initiating conversations with them through sincerity or out of our own selfish motives. In a discipling relationship, the disciple should take priority. We can help foster a relationship of trust by expressing authentic concern and care for an unbeliever. This sincerity promotes and encourages spiritual discussion. If we are not able to build a relationship with others in a spirit of authenticity, we should not be in the discipling business!

An example of someone who was deeply influenced by the authentic witness of his discipler was Francis. "This person was real about his faith," he said. "He didn't see his walk with God as perfect, nor did he expect that from anyone else. He was real about who God was and the expectations that came with being a Christian." Being authentic with unbelievers will enable them to feel comfortable sharing with us. Essentially, discipleship is a two-way street, because people can spiritually share with each other and learn from each other as partners in the gospel.

Expressing authenticity to people gives us opportunities to share what God has done for us. When we come to realize that he has rescued us from abusive relationships, provided support to us in times of needs, or loved us despite our many sins, we cannot help but be inexpressibly overcome with thankfulness, and share this with others. Gratitude will overpower any fear we may have of sharing the good news with others.

When we share intimately with others, they may ask us how we overcame certain struggles or how we can reconcile bad things that happen in our lives. How we address these issues will determine the influence we have on unbelievers. They are closely watching us and constantly evaluating our authenticity. Thus, as we engage in spiritual discussions with unbelievers we need to convey an attitude of sincerity and humility. When we can do this, the barriers of resistance are broken down and we are able to freely share the gospel with others. Our actions and attitudes will communicate more about Jesus than any sermon ever will!

THE CHALLENGE OF BEING AUTHENTIC

One of the best compliments I have received came from an unbelieving person. After he knew me for a while, he confessed, "You are not like other Christians I know. They seem so full of themselves and stuck-up. You are a real person." I had no idea he was sizing me up the whole time, but I was glad he came to that conclusion. Authenticity was the key.

Does it bother you that some people lump all disciples of Jesus into the same insincere group? You can change that misperception by following the example of authenticity Jesus set for us. If it is difficult for you to be transparent with others, your discipling influence on others will be limited. You can have a powerful impact on them if they know the real you—warts and all. If you are inconsistent in your actions, then you need to resolve it before you disciple others. Intentional discipleship requires us to lead lives that are consistent with the faith we profess.

If people do not view you as being authentic and real, you are not living dangerously! Authenticity has a dramatic effect on unbelievers. It shows them that you do not claim to be perfect and that you will not judge their imperfections. Being a person of authenticity leads others to Jesus!

QUESTIONS FOR DISCUSSION

- Why do you think unbelievers often view disciples of Jesus as insincere and hypocritical? Give some examples.

- Read Matthew 23:23–28. What does Jesus' admonition say to us today?

- Why is it important to be willing to admit to unbelievers when we're wrong or have weaknesses?

- Read Romans 3:23–24. Knowing that believers and unbelievers alike are sinners, what does that encourage you to share with unbelievers about Jesus?

- Why do you think authenticity fosters spiritual discussions with unbelievers?

PERSONAL REFLECTION

- Is there an area of your life in which your actions do not match your beliefs? What will you do about that?

- Pray that God will help you conquer any inconsistencies in your life and be able to authentically share the good news with others.

7

An Intentional Discipler Is Knowledgeable

The scriptures are given not to increase our knowledge,
but to change our lives.

—Dwight L. Moody

THE FOURTH KEY TO intentional discipleship is knowledge. When we demonstrate knowledge of the Scriptures to unbelievers, they are influenced to develop a relationship with Jesus. Throughout his ministry, Jesus exhibited his knowledge of the Scriptures by quoting from them numerous times. He was trained in the Scriptures when he was young, and his knowledge continued to grow as he matured. The apostle Luke said, "Jesus grew in wisdom and stature, and in favor with God and men" (Luke 2:52). The Scriptures were ingrained in Jesus' very being, and its words emanated from Jesus as he taught, healed, and prevailed over evil.

For instance, when Jesus was tempted in the desert, he drew strength from his well of Scripture knowledge to resist Satan. This account is recorded in Luke 4:3–12:

> The devil said to him, "If you are the Son of God, tell this stone to become bread." Jesus answered, "It is written: 'Man does not live on bread alone.'" The devil led him up to a high place and showed him in an instant all the kingdoms of the world. And he said to him, "I will give you all their authority and splendor, for it has been given to me, and I can give it to anyone I want to. So if you worship me, it will all be yours." Jesus answered, "It is written: 'Worship the Lord your God and serve him only.'" The devil led him to Jerusalem and had him stand on the highest point of the temple. "If you are the Son of God," he said, "throw yourself down from here. For it is written: 'He will command his angels concerning you to guard you carefully; they will lift you up in their hands, so that you will

not strike your foot against a stone.'" Jesus answered, "It says: 'Do not put the Lord your God to the test.'"

The application of Scripture was one of the trademarks of Jesus' ministry. He used the Scriptures to give him spiritual sustenance, power to resist temptation, and as a tool in discipling others. Jesus also understood the influence of Scriptures, and emphatically cited them. Matthew 7:29 says that Jesus imparted this knowledge "as one who had authority."

Just as Jesus dangerously used Scripture in his relationships with others, we can use knowledge to make disciples. The Scriptures contain vast storehouses of knowledge. Demonstrating this knowledge shows we are attuned to God's Word, and gives others confidence in our ability to disciple them. We need to continually keep God's Word at the forefront of our teaching. If our knowledge of Scriptures is lacking, we need to strengthen it to influence others. Through knowledge, others will be encouraged to give their lives to Jesus.

INFLUENCE OF KNOWLEDGE ON DISCIPLES

Disciplers who demonstrate knowledge influence unbelievers to give their lives to Jesus. The research revealed that both men and women were influenced by the knowledge of disciplers, but, when relatives were filtered out of the findings, women were influenced by knowledge to a higher degree than men. Figure 7.1 shows that women were impacted most by knowledge, followed by trustworthiness, care, faithfulness, authenticity, passion, and love.

Figure 7.1
Characteristics that had the biggest influence on women
(filtered without relatives)

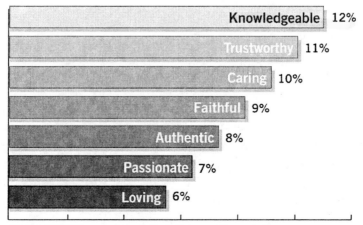

Knowledgeable	12%
Trustworthy	11%
Caring	10%
Faithful	9%
Authentic	8%
Passionate	7%
Loving	6%

The remaining 38% was comprised of traits that were of lesser significance.

Would we have expected knowledge to have the biggest impact on women? This disclosure flies in the face of those who suggest that women are more influenced by emotion while men are more influenced by logic. This is not the case in the conversion process.

Which gender of discipler displays knowledge to a higher degree? The overwhelming majority of disciplers who demonstrate knowledge are men. As Figure 7.2 shows, 82 percent of those who exhibited knowledge were men, while the remaining 18 percent were women.

Figure 7.2
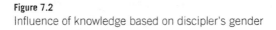
Influence of knowledge based on discipler's gender

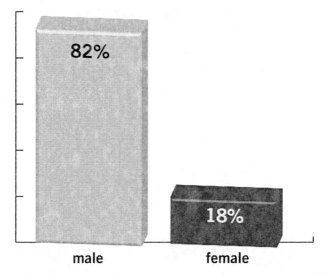

male   female

Statistically, this means that men were over four times more likely to demonstrate knowledge than women. Does this mean that men are more knowledgeable in the Scriptures than women? More conceivable explanations are that men are perceived to be more knowledgeable than women, or male disciplers display knowledge more often than women disciplers. At any rate, knowing that knowledge influences women to such a great extent gives disciplers incentive to portray this trait to women.

CHARACTERISTICS OF KNOWLEDGEABLE DISCIPLERS

Discerning if someone is knowledgeable seems obvious—either someone is familiar with the Scriptures or she is not. Nevertheless, unbelievers indicated that there were explicit indications of knowledgeable disciplers. They revealed that knowledgeable disciplers studied the Word of God, made the Scriptures relevant, and welcomed biblical questions.

A Knowledgeable Discipler Studies the Word

I cannot remember a day that I did not see my father reading from the Bible. He would sometimes sit for hours at a time reflecting on its message. As a child, I can remember thinking, "How boring! Hasn't he read that part already"? Without uttering a word, my father taught me that consistent Bible study was a discipline I needed to cultivate.

Studying the Word of God is a practical way to demonstrate scriptural knowledge to others. Unbelievers relayed the connection between Bible study and knowledge. Kimberly said that her discipler "studied and read his Bible a lot. He was able to show me the Scriptures in anything that he told me." Similarly, Sheri said, "He read the Bible and knew that was where we meet God and find what He has to say."

As made apparent in these comments, influential disciplers spend time reading the Bible. If we are steeped in the Scriptures, God's words flow effortlessly from our lips. We need to intentionally study the Scriptures in preparation for discipleship. Paul told Timothy, "All Scripture is God-breathed and is useful for teaching, rebuking, correcting and training in righteousness, so that the man of God may be thoroughly equipped for every good work" (2 Tim 3:16–17). The Scriptures give us the knowledge to teach others because they are the inspired words of God. One way that God speaks to us and unbelievers is through his Word.

Unbelievers also observed a link between knowledge and authenticity. Chris said, "He reads many books, studies the Bible daily. He doesn't believe at first glance, because he constantly seeks the truth even if it shakes his own faith foundation." When we earnestly study the Scriptures, our conversations with others communicate sincerity and a sense of legitimacy.

If we are not spending a substantial amount of time reading and studying the Word, we need to refocus our energy into boosting that discipline. Immersing ourselves in Scripture is a valuable means of increasing our knowledge and influencing unbelievers.

A Knowledgeable Discipler Makes Scripture Relevant

Some factual knowledge is essential in making disciples, but what seems to matter more to them is our ability to make the Bible relevant to their lives. One way to begin making the Bible relevant to unbelievers is to find out what they know about Scripture, and then build upon their knowledge. I have studied with unbelievers who knew the Bible as well as any seminary graduate, but I have also met some people who did not know where to find the book of Genesis. Meeting unbelievers where they are is always an expedient motto to embrace.

Making Scripture relevant also means having the ability to understand the Scriptures and explain it to unbelievers. Kathy said, "The person was knowledgeable because he gave examples from the Bible that would help me with my faith and encourage me to give my life to Christ."

Knowledge is valuable when we can make practical applications of Scripture—to connect real issues to God's Word. People who have suffered the loss of a loved one, sustained abuse of some kind, or have experienced the pain of failed relationships need the encouragement that comes from God's Word. Sonny said, "He could answer all my questions by pointing to the Word to let God's wisdom change my heart and give me direction."

When we disciple others, we need to be able to discern the needs of unbelievers and guide them to experience the healing and transformational power of Scripture. The Bible is chock-full of passages that are relevant to people today. Genesis reveals the care God provides; many of the psalms demonstrate the strength that God freely gives; and most of the Proverbs contain helpful pieces of wisdom.

Knowing Scripture well gives us the ability to make direct applications of God's Word to the lives of unbelievers. If God's Word is planted deep in our hearts, we will be able to instantly recall passages that relate to the individual needs of unbelievers. Consistent Bible study is one way that Scripture can permeate our hearts and minds. Another useful way to make God's Word relevant to others is by memorizing Scripture. This does not have to be mindless repetition; memorization can be part of our daily routines. For example, we can write out Scriptures on paper and post them in obvious places around the house. We can also place Scriptures in inconspicuous places in our office, such as our desk drawers. This method is especially useful for remembering some of our favorite passages. The idea is to let God's Word seep into our thoughts so thoroughly that we will be able to automatically cite relevant Scriptures in discussions with unbelievers.

A Knowledgeable Discipler Welcomes Questions

Disciplers were also perceived as being influential on unbelievers when they took the time and energy to address specific biblical questions. Peter described the necessity of addressing biblical questions in 1 Peter 3:15: "Always be prepared to give an answer to everyone who asks you to give the reason for the hope that you have. But do this with gentleness and respect."

One of the biggest obstacles we need to overcome in making disciples is resistance to spiritual discussions. Questions should never threaten us in any way. Chloe said of her discipler, "If he couldn't answer my questions, he would do some research and get back to me. He wasn't scared off by my questions." If we do not have all the answers, unbelievers will understand we are not perfect. We can always seek answers to their questions and get back to them later. What counts more than having all the answers is having the fortitude to stick with people as we disciple them. We need to remember we are not the only ones who are investing time—unbelievers are too.

One good way to address spiritual questions is to show unbelievers examples from the Bible. Bruce said that his discipler "always answered questions with specific Bible references." Tonya agreed. "He always had an answer to any question I had, and knew where to find it in the Bible." We need to dig into the Scriptures as we discuss spiritual matters and let God's Word speak to us.

Spending time in the Scriptures prepares us to respond to questions that will inevitably arise in the discipleship process. We need to equip ourselves for this task. Welcoming questions means more than simply relaying information. The process also requires an attitude of humility. Connie said, "She would answer my questions, and wasn't afraid to admit she didn't know the answer but would look it up." Most of us are not Bible scholars, and do not always have the facts at our fingertips. If an unbeliever asks us a question we cannot immediately answer, it is okay to humbly admit our ignorance and research the answer together. Studying the Scriptures with an unbeliever can actually increase our own biblical knowledge.

It is easy to become defensive when people question our faith, but we need to have faith that God will guide our responses. When Jesus instructed his disciples how to defend their faith, he encouraged them by saying, "do not worry about how you will defend yourselves or what you will say, for the Holy Spirit will teach you at that time what you should say" (Luke 12:12–13). Engaging in spiritual dialogue with others can be a frightening experience, but God will show us exactly what to say at the right time.

No one has all the answers. Unbelievers will probably have questions we cannot answer, and they may likely confront us by asking questions that challenge our theology. It is easy to be discouraged by questions that seem threatening to our way of understanding. We need to remember that discipleship is a mutually beneficial relationship: we can learn as much from unbelievers as they can learn from us. Therefore, our responsibility is to set a tone of openness by providing a safe environment. Intentional discipleship involves developing our knowledge and conveying it with humility and patience.

THE CHALLENGE OF BEING KNOWLEDGEABLE

Do you have a solid knowledge of the Scriptures? That is, are you armed with the sword of the Spirit well enough to answer the questions that unbelievers may ask you? No matter how complete your Bible knowledge is, you can likely stand to bolster your knowledge of God's Word. I have known many ministers who spend so much time studying for sermons or classes that they neglect meditating on Scriptures for their own spiritual growth. If we are not regularly feeding on God's Word, we will be ill-equipped for sharing Scripture with others.

Are you able to show others how to understand and study the Bible? You do not need to have a degree in advanced hermeneutics or exegesis, but you do need to have a grasp of how the Scriptures are organized, and how to interpret them. These are valuable Bible study tools you can pass on to others. If you have not developed a Bible study system of your own, there are many beneficial resources that can help you study and analyze the Scriptures.

Disciplers who dangerously demonstrate their knowledge of the Scriptures influence unbelievers. The Word of God is a powerful means by which God speaks to people today. Psalm 119:105 says, "Your word is a lamp to my feet and a light for my path." God's Word will give light to unbelievers and help them see his face. Our job is to lead unbelievers to Jesus by studying the Scriptures, making God's Word relevant to their circumstances, and preparing ourselves to answer any biblical questions that may arise. Are you ready for this incredible task?

QUESTIONS FOR DISCUSSION

- What part did Scripture play in your own conversion? What part does it still play in your spiritual walk?

- Why did Jesus use Scripture to overcome Satan's temptations? Is this an example we should follow? Why or why not?

- Read 2 Timothy 3:16–17. In what ways do the Scriptures equip us to make disciples?

- Read 1 Peter 3:15. What are some ways we can respond to an unbeliever's questions with gentleness and respect?

- In Luke 12:12, Jesus said that the Holy Spirit would guide us as we talk with unbelievers. How does this work? Do you trust God to do this?

PERSONAL REFLECTION

- Do you study the Scriptures outside of Bible classes? If not, make a commitment to find times this week to regularly feed and meditate on God's Word.

- Pray that you will trust in God's guidance as you discuss the Scriptures with unbelievers.

8

An Intentional Discipler Is Trustworthy

Don't trust to hold God's hand; let Him hold yours.
Let Him do the holding, and you the trusting.

—HAMMER WILLIAM WEBB-PEPLOE

THE FIFTH KEY TO intentional discipleship is trustworthiness. Jesus was trustworthy. One of the reasons people trusted him is because he knew how to be discreet if the situation demanded it. One of the best examples of Jesus' trustworthiness is found in John's gospel account.

In John chapter three, a man named Nicodemus came to Jesus at night. Nicodemus was a Pharisee, but more than that, he was a member of the Jewish ruling council—the Sanhedrin. As a member of this council, Nicodemus had dedicated his life to upholding Jewish laws and religious traditions.

Why did Nicodemus come at night? By the types of questions he asked, it is apparent that Nicodemus earnestly desired to more fully understand spiritual truths. It is possible that he went to Jesus at night because he wanted to avoid the crowds that gathered around Jesus during the day, but the context seems to suggest that—because of his position— Nicodemus did not want to be seen talking with Jesus. There is every indication that Nicodemus met with Jesus because he trusted him, and because he knew Jesus would keep Nicodemus's identity confidential.

This encounter with Jesus left a permanent impression on Nicodemus. Later in Jesus' ministry, when the Pharisees sent guards to arrest Jesus and they returned without him, Nicodemus asked them, "Does our law condemn anyone without first hearing him to find out what he is doing?" (John 7:51). His changed outlook affected him, causing him to stand up for Jesus in the face of adversity.

After Jesus was crucified, Nicodemus helped Joseph of Arimathea prepare Jesus' body for burial (John 19:39). He did this knowing that it might jeopardize his position with the Sanhedrin.

When Jesus dangerously displayed trustworthiness to Nicodemus, he responded to Jesus' words and his life was transformed. Similarly, when we demonstrate trustworthiness to others, they become receptive to the gospel and are influenced to give their lives to Jesus.

Trust is integral to effective discipling relationships. In a world of electronic babysitters and cyber chatting, it is sometimes difficult to build close, trusting relationships with others. We cannot disciple by remote control. Making disciples is an interactive, face-to-face process that takes time to develop. Making disciples can naturally happen when we have a relationship of trust with someone.

Discipling others is a deeply personal process that requires the exchange of spiritual concerns. This cannot be accomplished unless we are trustworthy. I know unbelievers who are more trustworthy than some of my Christian brothers and sisters. We need to follow the example of Jesus by being a trustworthy person.

INFLUENCE OF TRUSTWORTHINESS ON DISCIPLES

Disciplers who demonstrate trustworthiness influence unbelievers to commit their lives to Jesus. The research revealed that unbelievers were more likely to be influenced by relatives who demonstrated trustworthiness than by any other type of relationship. As figure 8.1 indicates, 50 percent of all disciplers who exhibited trustworthiness were related to unbelievers, 27 percent of disciplers were ministers, 18 percent were friends, and 5 percent of disciplers were comprised of various other kinds of relationships.

Figure 8.1
Influence of trustworthiness based on relationship

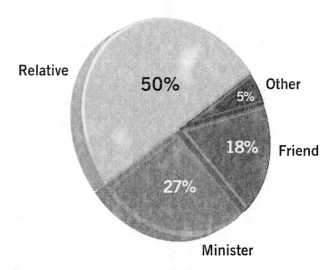

It is not striking to notice that relatives of unbelievers portray high levels of trust to them. This reveals the significance relatives play in making disciples. If we are related to unbelievers, trust is a crucial trait that we must develop and implement in our relationships with them.

Trust also differs according to gender. The research revealed that trustworthiness influenced unbelievers who were both male and female. However, as revealed in chapter seven, trust had a greater impact on women than men. When trust can be established between a discipler and an unbelieving person, the door will be opened wide for discipling to begin.

Statistically speaking, men were perceived as being over three times more likely than women to demonstrate trustworthiness. Figure 8.2 shows that 77 percent of disciplers who exhibited trustworthiness were men, and 23 percent were women.

Figure 8.2
Influence of trustworthiness based on discipler's gender

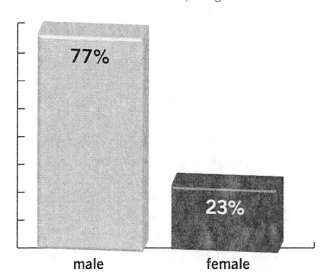

male   female

This suggests that male disciplers need to be aware of their influence on others by being trustworthy. Further, this result challenges women to build deeper levels of trust in their relationships with others.

CHARACTERISTICS OF TRUSTWORTHY DISCIPLES

Trustworthiness can be defined in several ways. To gain a better understanding of how trust is involved in discipling relationships, unbelievers were asked to give an example of how their disciplers were trustworthy. The results revealed that a trustworthy discipler maintains confidentiality, has integrity, and is honest.

A Trustworthy Discipler Maintains Confidentiality

Disciplers are viewed as being trustworthy when they maintain confidentiality in their interactions with unbelievers. We have all had the experience of sharing personal information with someone, expecting him to keep it confidential, only to discover later that he has relayed our secrets to others. Just as Jesus maintained confidentiality with Nicodemus, we need to respect the privacy of unbelievers and keep their personal matters to ourselves.

Maintaining confidence with unbelievers promotes trustworthy discipling relationships, and influences them to share personal issues with us. A representative remark was made by Toni, who said, "I could tell him anything about my personal life and know it was just between us." It is often very difficult for unbelievers to share personal struggles and concerns with others, especially when they are spiritual in nature. As disciplers, our responsibility is to keep personal matters private, and assure unbelievers that we can maintain confidentiality.

Unbelievers also need to know they can trust us enough to share personal issues with us. Serena said, "He was always someone that I could trust to know and understand what he claimed to be true. I felt that he would never mislead me in any way because he always wanted what was best for me." If unbelievers trust their disciplers, they are more apt to believe their discipler's assertions about Jesus, and what he has done for them. As disciplers, we need to be cognizant of the trust factor in the discipling relationship, and exhibit trust in our actions and words.

Unbelievers need to know we can keep secrets. Many of them have been betrayed and hurt by others, and find it difficult to trust anyone. When we establish relationships with unbelievers, we can replace these negative experiences with trustworthy actions. They need to feel secure knowing that we will never divulge their innermost fears and struggles to others.

A Trustworthy Discipler Has Integrity

Unbelievers are also influenced by people who have personal integrity. A person with integrity is dependable and means what he says. It means having strength of character, and leading a life that is beyond reproach. We live in a world that justifies deceitfulness and backbiting if these actions help achieve greater fame, fortune, or social status. The prevailing sentiment seems to be that it does not matter who we hurt as long as we come out ahead. Unbelievers have endured this narrow, hurtful thinking for too long, and have grown accustomed to second-guessing even good-willed people. We can offer healing and safety to unbelievers by showing them integrity.

Disciplers who demonstrate integrity lead unbelievers to Jesus. Francine said, "I know when he says something, he means it." This simple statement says a lot. It shows a need to associate with someone who is dependable and stable. Additionally, it indicates the importance of being in a relationship that is built on trust. If we mean what we say, others will be able to depend on us, and the discipling relationship will grow.

Unbelievers are also impacted by people who keep their word. Antoine felt his discipler was trustworthy. "He could be counted on to keep his word," he said. Keeping our word does not give unbelievers false hopes or promises, but demonstrates our loyalty in the discipling relationship. When this happens, unbelievers are drawn into trusting relationships with us.

Making disciples is such an incredible task that we cannot afford to miss out on opportunities by being anything less than trustworthy. Integrity is not merely skin-deep. It is a virtue that is developed from the inside out. When we model Jesus by displaying integrity in our discipling relationships, others will be influenced to establish a trustworthy relationship with Jesus.

A *Trustworthy Discipler Is Honest*

Honesty is another aspect of trust that influences unbelievers to develop a relationship with Jesus. How many times have people lied to us? Probably more than we want to know. It would be difficult to imagine someone being trustworthy if he or she was not honest. "My discipler would never lie to me," said Nora. "We have a very close relationship. I knew that if she didn't know something, she wouldn't just make it up and answer, but offer to discover the answer with me. I always knew she would tell me the truth to the best of her possible knowledge."

Being honest also implies a level of genuineness. There is nothing that will put a halt to a discipling relationship faster than misrepresenting the truth—particularly spiritual truth. Steve said, "He was always someone I could trust to know and understand what he claimed to be true. I felt he would never mislead me in any way because he always wanted what was best for me."

Some unbelievers have been hurt so many times that they no longer trust anyone. After experiencing dishonest parents, deceitful relationships, and untrustworthy employers, we may be the first people to tell unbelievers the truth. The great thing is that we know the truth! Jesus said that "the truth will set you free" (John 8:32). When we are truthful with unbelievers, and they come to trust in Jesus, they will be set free from their distrustful lives!

Being dishonest with someone betrays a friendship and jeopardizes our potential influence in the discipling relationship. Conversely, honesty promotes a relationship of mutual trust and sincerity. If honesty does not come naturally to us, that inadequacy needs to be corrected before we can effectively disciple others. Honesty is an intentional portrayal of our discipling motives.

TRUST FOSTERS SPIRITUAL DISCUSSIONS

Unbelievers who were led to Jesus through a discipling relationship were asked, "Why did you feel comfortable discussing spiritual matters with this person?" They indicated that they were comfortable engaging in spiritual discussions with someone who was trustworthy. Trust was highlighted by unbelievers as fostering spiritual discussion because they felt that disciplers supported them and offered them security. Jenna said, "He didn't make me feel like I was inadequate; rather, that I had something to offer."

Everyone likes to feel valued and competent. Too often, people have been verbally abused in some way or they have lost confidence in themselves, leaving them with a feeling of inadequacy. We know that Jesus cares for these people because all people are precious to him (1 Peter 2:4). Jesus is seeking unbelievers who are struggling with feelings of low self-worth! He wants to hold them and love them. We can support unbelievers by leading them to the One who considers them to be precious and valuable.

Unbelievers also feel comfortable having spiritual discussions with people who offer them security. Ben said, "He's a safe guy . . . I know that even if I have every thing wrong, he's still going to care about me." Similarly, Toby said, "This person was safe and understanding."

It is reassuring to talk with people who provide security in a relationship. When we interact with these kinds of people, we naturally feel less inhibited to share personal or confidential information with them. For some, this may be a liberating experience. When unbelievers trust us enough to have intimate spiritual discussions with us, they begin to understand the security and safety that Jesus provides. If we desire to engage in spiritual conversations with unbelievers, we need to demonstrate trustworthiness.

THE CHALLENGE OF BEING TRUSTWORTHY

Developing relationships of trust with unbelievers can be a monumental task. After all, we, as Christians, have let people down for more than a thousand years by our cruel and arrogant behavior. In the middle ages, Christians who were seeking spiritual cleansing killed thousands of innocent people during the crusades and inquisitions. Later, Christians killed many people in the name of God during the witch trials. Christians also justified the hangings and mistreatment of many slaves in the United States. More recently, Christians have bombed abortion clinics and have attacked others during demonstrations. Although not all Christians were involved in these atrocities, these actions have given Christianity a bad name, and have caused many to be cynical and distrustful of Jesus followers. Is it any wonder that some people have such a negative view of Christians?

Trust may be the biggest obstacle unbelievers will have to overcome before they can develop a relationship with Jesus. We need to be trustworthy disciples; but beyond that, we can help others put their trust in Jesus. He said, "Do not let your hearts be troubled. Trust in God; trust also in me" (John 14:1). We must communicate to unbelievers that God cares for them, and he will never let them down.

Are you trustworthy? If you are not, you will not be an effective discipler. Far too many unbelievers have been hurt by Christians who did not recognize the value of trust in relationships. This has driven many people far from potentially healthy relationships. We have been given opportunities to show unbelievers that God wants to be in a relationship with them. We can intentionally demonstrate trustworthiness to them by maintaining a sense of confidentiality, having personal integrity, and exhibiting honesty. Dangerously exhibiting trust will draw others to Jesus, and he will soothe their pain, heal their aches, and lovingly comfort them.

QUESTIONS FOR DISCUSSION

- Describe a time when you have been betrayed. Was it difficult to trust that person? Explain.

- Read John 3:1–21. What did Jesus say and do that helped Nicodemus trust him?

- Why do you think unbelievers are influenced by someone who has the ability to maintain confidentiality with them?

- Read John 14:1. How is this passage comforting for unbelievers?

- What are some practical ways that we, as Christians, can build trusting relationships with unbelievers?

PERSONAL REFLECTION

- Are you honest with people? Can they trust you to keep their personal thoughts confidential? If not, it could be that you do not trust God to take control of your life. Submit yourself to his guidance and leading.

- Pray that God will show you how to increase your trustworthiness.

9

An Intentional Discipler Is Caring

God cares about the big things and the little things in our lives.
No matter what.

—JOHN HULL

THE SIXTH KEY TO intentional discipleship is care. Jesus expressed care to people throughout his ministry. One of the most striking depictions of care is exemplified in John's gospel account. As Jesus was traveling through Samaria, he stopped at a well to get a drink of water and recuperate. When a Samaritan woman came to the well, Jesus initiated a conversation with her. He said, "Will you give me a drink?" (John 4:7). The woman responded in John 4:9, "You are a Jew and I am a Samaritan woman. How can you ask me for a drink? (For Jews do not associate with Samaritans.)"

Talking with a Samaritan was extraordinary for two main reasons. First, Jews did not associate with Samaritans because they had a mixed heritage: Israelites and foreigners. As such, Samaritans were considered "half-breeds." Second, Jews did not tolerate Samaritans because they were religiously pluralistic—they worshipped both God and idols. Thus, Jews considered Samaritans to be detestable, and avoided them at all costs. Jesus ignored these social mores. He was not racist, nor did he judge people based on their religious preferences.

Additionally, it was also highly unusual for a man to speak to a woman. In Jesus' time, women were regarded as subordinate to men. They were not allowed to vote or act as witnesses in court, and they were not allowed to speak to men in public. Jesus broke the gender barrier and demonstrated genuine care to the woman by speaking to her.

Later in the conversation between Jesus and the woman, Jesus revealed that she had been married five times—or at least that she had been with five men. Nevertheless, Jesus never judged the woman for her lifestyle; instead, he extended his care to her by offering her living water. The woman did not understand, and stated, "I know that Messiah" (called Christ) "is coming. When he comes, he will explain everything to us" (John 4:25). Jesus answered her, "I who speak to you am he" (John 4:26). This is, in fact, the first time Jesus revealed himself as the Messiah.

The narrative does not end with the conversation between Jesus and the woman. Jesus' care for her caused a snowball effect. The woman went back to her city and told her people about Jesus. Then the Samaritans invited Jesus to the city, where he stayed for two days. As a result of Jesus' dangerous care for the Samaritans, many of them became believers! When Jesus cared for people, they were deeply touched and responded with belief. Likewise, when we intentionally demonstrate care to people, they will see Jesus in us and come to know him.

Jesus can empathize with us because he became human and lived among us. The writer of Hebrews says, "For we do not have a high priest who is unable to sympathize with our weaknesses, but we have one who has been tempted in every way, just as we are—yet was without sin" (Heb 4:15). Jesus cares for us because he understands what we go through every day. He knows the temptations we face, the heartaches we bear, and the hopes we anticipate. When we hurt, Jesus hurts with us and comforts us; when we fall into sin, he picks us up and wipes off the dirt; when we are sad, he embraces us in his loving arms. He calls us sons, children, and heirs. We do not have some ethereal lord in the sky who created us, and then left us alone. He is an active participant in our lives! To be intentional disciplers, we need to follow the example of Jesus and dangerously demonstrate care to others.

INFLUENCE OF CARE ON DISCIPLES

The research revealed that care was more likely to be demonstrated by friends of unbelievers than by any other type of relationship. As figure 9.1 illustrates, 36 percent of all disciplers who demonstrated care were friends of unbelievers; 31 percent were relatives, 18 percent were ministers, and the remaining 15 percent was comprised of various other kinds of relationships.

Figure 9.1
Influence of caring based on relationship

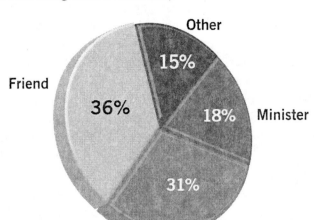

This correlation should not be interpreted as reflecting poorly on relatives, ministers, or any other kinds of relationships. It purely means that friends are people who are most often perceived as being caring. Although friends of unbelievers do not have the highest influence on them overall, it is helpful to know that friends have the greatest influence when they demonstrate care to others.

CHARACTERISTICS OF CARING DISCIPLERS

Exhibiting care influences others to commit their lives to Jesus. Unbelievers who were influenced by caring disciplers were asked to give an example of how their disciplers exhibited care. The results revealed that disciplers who influenced unbelievers listened to them, were giving of their time, and were patient with them.

A Caring Discipler Listens

The first way an intentional discipler exhibits care to unbelievers is by listening to them. I met a homeless man a few years ago who was lonely and depressed. We began talking and forged a relationship. Almost from the beginning, I realized that this man needed someone to talk to; someone who would listen to him. I asked him to tell me his story—and he talked!

For sometimes hours at a time, he talked and I listened to his sad—but fascinating—life. We were good for each other: his stories captivated me, and he desperately needed someone to talk to. After a while we began talking about spiritual matters; and ultimately, he decided to follow Jesus. After he was baptized, he told me that I was his "spiritual father," although he was older than me! I am convinced that he came to know Christ because I took time to listen.

Listening is an integral ingredient in making disciples. Elliott put it succinctly. "He listened to me. He cared about me." When we listen to people talk about matters dear to their hearts, we are interpreted as being caring. Listening to others lets them vent their frustrations and fears, and it encourages spiritual dialogue.

Listening requires a degree of intensity. A universal remark made by unbelievers was that a caring discipler is one who lets people talk about problems they may have, and listens attentively to them. Pam said, "She was willing to just listen to my concerns." Listening is a learned behavior; it does not come naturally. It is important to listen to others without continually thinking about what we are going to say. We need to listen without feeling compelled to add our two cents. True listening allows others to express their personal concerns without fear of rebuttal or judgment.

One good way to practice listening is by asking people open-ended questions. These are questions that require more than a yes or no, and evoke thoughtful responses. Then, our job is to listen to them without condemnation. Sometimes, people just need to feel free to express themselves. This is even more crucial in spiritual discussions with people. They need to freely express their spiritual beliefs to us without being attacked. Our role is to listen to them with open minds. If we disagree with something they say, we can gently address it when the time is right.

If unbelievers trust us, they will likely feel compelled to share personal stories with us. It is crucial that we provide an environment that encourages—instead of discourages—these intimate revelations. Unbelievers need to know that they can express their feelings, their fears, and their spiritual concerns freely to us without being ridiculed or mocked in any way. Sometimes, people just need someone to listen to them. Listening shows that we care and that we are concerned for unbelievers. We need to develop the habit of active listening.

A Caring Discipler Is Giving

Unbelievers also revealed that caring disciplers gave time to unbelievers. A friend of mine experienced the benefits of giving time to someone. She became friends with a man who was bedridden, and was unable to do many tasks by himself. My friend was determined to find a way to minister to the man, and decided to spend time clipping his toenails. She took time to express this care for the man regularly for a year. After the man died, his wife and daughter began attending church with my friend; and later, the man's son and daughter-in-law began attending. Eventually, they all committed their lives to Jesus. All of this was made possible by a woman who gave of herself to perform such a simple act as clipping toenails!

Disciplers who exhibit care influence others to follow Jesus. Giving our time to unbelievers is a vital ingredient of making disciples. Bill said, "He made time to talk with me and tried to lead the conversation into my relationship with Jesus through a situation I was telling him about." Exhibiting care takes time. When we give our most valuable resource to others, they will know that the care we express to them is sincere.

Taking time involves more than being with others; it means that we freely give our time to them. Tara said, "She would give of herself and her time to see to the needs of another person." Giving ourselves to others should never be a burden or a difficult task. Giving is a natural outgrowth of the love we have for them.

Giving time to unbelievers also means that we prioritize them in our schedules. We know that Jesus left his simple life in Nazareth to disciple others. In Matthew 18:12–14, he compared his compassion for the lost to a shepherd who forsakes all else to look for his lost sheep: "If a man owns a hundred sheep, and one of them wanders away, will he not leave the ninety-nine on the hills and go to look for the one that wandered off? And if he finds it, I tell you the truth, he is happier about that one sheep than about the ninety-nine that did not wander off. In the same way your Father in heaven is not willing that any of these little ones should be lost."

We are called to make disciples, and sometimes this requires us to abandon ninety-nine pet projects or distractions to fulfill our mission. We may think we are already too busy to disciple others, but a hurried life that takes us away from our singular purpose in life does not help anyone. In America, being busy is practically synonymous with being successful. Busyness does not get us anywhere, unless we are living dangerously.

Before we begin discipling others, we need to ask ourselves if we are willing to make another person a priority in our lives. An intentional discipler is like a medical doctor or minister: he or she is always on call. Giving time to unbelievers means that we will always be willing to respond to their needs. If we desire to become intentional disciplers, it will take a decisive commitment on our part to give our time to others.

A Caring Discipler Is Patient

Another way to demonstrate care to unbelievers is by being patient with them. The word "tolerance" has been overused by both sides of the political spectrum. Nevertheless, making disciples requires us to be tolerant of others. Unbelievers will challenge us in many different ways. They may have diverse spiritual beliefs, theological misunderstandings or they may lead lifestyles that are completely foreign to us. Being patient with them will help them see Jesus in us. This does not mean that we have to blindly accept their beliefs or actions; it means that we have to be patient as the Holy Spirit works in their lives.

Being patient with people allows God to work in their lives. Psalm 37:7 says, "Be still before the Lord and wait patiently for him." April knew that her discipler cared for her. "He prayed with me," she said, "even when I wanted to do it multiple times." God has his own sense of timing. He will work in the lives of unbelievers when the circumstances are right. However, if we are not patient in discipling others, we limit God's ability to use us.

When we develop caring relationships with others, sooner or later spiritual matters will arise. When they do, we need to maintain a healthy outlook and patiently express our care to them. Sally said, "She was patient with my questions that may have seemed dumb to others." Patience expresses care because it shows others that we take their spiritual concerns seriously—without judging the person.

Patience is not only a virtue; it is a necessary ingredient in making disciples. Patience is not an innate quality, but it can be cultivated. Although it is sometimes difficult to put into practice, our patience influences others to be receptive to the gospel.

CARING FOSTERS SPIRITUAL DISCUSSIONS

Unbelievers who were led to Jesus through a discipling relationship were asked, "Why did you feel comfortable discussing spiritual matters with this person?" They responded that they felt comfortable discussing spiritual matters with disciplers because they were caring. Disciplers demonstrated care by listening, being patient, and expressing interest in the welfare of unbelievers.

Madeline disclosed that her discipler listened to her. "I could pour out my soul to her and she always listened," she said. Likewise, Terry said, "She knew me my whole life and was always willing to listen to me and answer my questions." Listening to people shows them that we are concerned about them on an intimate level. It helps them feel safe sharing their innermost thoughts, desires, and dreams with us.

Devon said his discipler exhibited a caring attitude by exercising patience. "He was wise, kind, and patient," he said. "He never made me feel silly for asking questions or having a problem." Cheri said she felt comfortable having spiritual discussions with her discipler because he was patient with her. "This man let me express myself, befriended me, and was patient with me," she said. Discipling others necessitates having perseverance and demonstrating patience to another person, even when they ask questions that we may consider elementary. On the other hand, unbelievers may ask questions that are totally foreign to us and challenge our thinking. No matter what questions we are asked, we need to be prepared to patiently answer them.

Unbelievers also were open to discussing spiritual matters with disciplers who exhibited genuine interest in their welfare. Brad said, "He was easy to talk to and always seemed interested in me and what was going on in my life." Bernie echoed this sentiment. He said, "He cared about what was going on in my life and was willing to help me become a better person for God."

Care is demonstrated to unbelievers when we sincerely show personal interest in their struggles, heartaches, and dreams. If others know that we care for them and desire the best for their lives, they will be prompted to share spiritual matters with us. This is not something we can fake. We should only express care for unbelievers if we are fully interested in developing an honest relationship with them.

THE CHALLENGE OF BEING CARING

Jesus showed us the heart of God through his attitudes and actions. He is not an emotionless, stoic god who delights in our weaknesses, but a caring God who empathizes with our sorrows. Psalm 34:18 tells us, "The Lord is close to the brokenhearted and saves those who are crushed in spirit." We are able to exhibit care for others because God first expressed care to us. Many people have not experienced care in their lives, and need the life-sustaining warmth that it provides.

Are you willing to listen to others without judging them? Are you prepared to prioritize others by making them an integral part of your agenda? Are you a patient person? A caring discipler is able and willing to demonstrate all three qualities to others.

Just as Jesus offered care to people who were despised by many others, you need to express care to unbelievers. For those who are spiritually broken as a result of uncaring and thoughtless people in their lives, you may be the first person that offers them sincere care. Your task is to dangerously care for unbelievers. Doing so will draw them into the sweet, healing embrace of Jesus.

QUESTIONS FOR DISCUSSION

- Describe a time that you were aware of God's care for you.

- Read Hebrews 4:15. In what ways does this verse illustrate that Jesus cares for us?

- How does listening to unbelievers demonstrate care?

- Read Matthew 18:12-14. What is Jesus telling us about seeking those who are lost? What things get in the way of doing this?

- In what ways does answering an unbeliever's questions demonstrate care to him?

PERSONAL REFLECTION

- Are you ready to invest a substantial amount of your time with unbelievers? If not, what can you change about yourself to prepare for this monumental task?

- Pray that God will give you the patience and concern necessary for building relationships with unbelievers.

10

An Intentional Discipler Is Passionate

I have but one passion. 'Tis He, only He.

—Count Zinzendorf

THE SEVENTH KEY TO intentional discipleship is passion. Jesus lived passionately, and he demonstrated his passion at a young age. When Jesus was only twelve years old, he and his family were in Jerusalem for the Passover. After the Passover, Jesus stayed in Jerusalem, unbeknownst to his family. The family had already traveled a day before they realized he was not with them. They went back and found Jesus talking with the teachers of the law. Luke 2:47–49 indicates what happened: "Everyone who heard him was amazed at his understanding and his answers. When his parents saw him, they were astonished. His mother said to him, "Son, why have you treated us like this? Your father and I have been anxiously searching for you." "Why were you searching for me?" he asked. "Didn't you know I had to be in my Father's house?" Even at twelve, Jesus was so passionate about his mission that he nearly neglected his own family.

Jesus also demonstrated passion when his friend Lazarus died. John 11:32–35 reveals Jesus' emotions: "When Mary reached the place where Jesus was and saw him, she fell at his feet and said, 'Lord, if you had been here, my brother would not have died.' When Jesus saw her weeping, and the Jews who had come along with her also weeping, he was deeply moved in spirit and troubled. 'Where have you laid him?' he asked. 'Come and see, Lord,' they replied. Jesus wept." He felt empathy for Lazarus' sisters and friends when they wept over Lazarus. Jesus eventually was no longer able to compose himself and wept. Jesus was overcome with emotion because he was a passionate person.

Jesus also uttered words that plainly revealed his passion. On several occasions, he called the Pharisees a "brood of vipers." He drove out the money changers in the temple, and he grieved over the lost in Jerusalem (Luke 13:34).

Jesus lived passionately by throwing himself into everything he did. Similarly, we are called to be like Jesus by interjecting energy into our discipling mission and exuding excitement for Jesus to unbelievers. When we do, they will be influenced to give their lives to Jesus.

Do we really believe that people who do not know Jesus are lost? If we do, we need to put our beliefs into practice by passionately discipling others! When we live like this, our lives will be anything but boring! Living passionately means that we would die for our faith. Being passionate is living dangerously!

INFLUENCE OF PASSION ON DISCIPLES

How is passion defined? Passion is such an intangible, abstract quality that it is difficult to measure. However, we are easily able to spot those who are passionate. The research has shown that disciplers who live passionately have a transforming impact on unbelievers. Passionate disciplers initiate spiritual dialogue early in their relationships with unbelievers. Figure 10.1 reveals that 64 percent of passionate disciplers initiated conversations with Jesus within three months after meeting an unbeliever. Only 27 percent of passionate disciplers waited more than a year to bring up Jesus in conversation. This is logical, since a passionate person is more likely to act on his or her spiritual fervor.

Figure 10.1

Influence of passion based on how long until Jesus was brought up in conversation

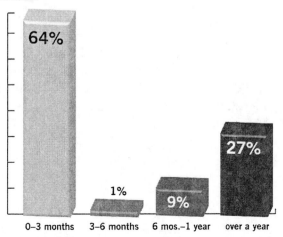

What kind of relationship is likely to display passion the most? As Figure 10.2 shows, 36 percent of passionate disciplers were ministers, followed by 26 percent who were relatives, and 25 percent who were friends. The remaining 13 percent of disciplers was comprised of various other relationships.

Figure 10.2
Influence of passion based on relationship

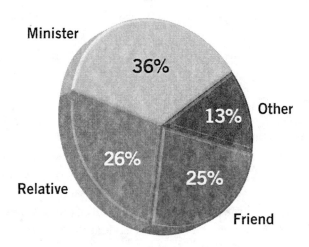

The data suggest that ministers are conveying passion very well—at least in the amount of time it took to initiate spiritual conversations. This should not be construed as a weakness for disciplers who are not ministers. There are certainly other traits that are effective in making disciples. It may be that demonstrating passion is easier for those who have been called to ministry.

CHARACTERISTICS OF PASSIONATE DISCIPLERS

Since passion is an inward emotion, how do we express it to others? Unbelievers who were influenced by passion were asked to give an example of how their disciplers were passionate. The results revealed that disciplers demonstrated passion by being devoted to Jesus, being enthusiastic about him, and by being driven to share the gospel with others.

A Passionate Discipler Is Devoted

As indicated by unbelievers, a passionate person is one who is devoted to Jesus. I have a friend who is not afraid to express his devotion to God. Every time someone compliments him, he responds with, "Praise God!" And he says the same thing when anyone tells him about an answered prayer. He looks for opportunities to share his passion for God, and it does not matter where he is or who hears him. For him, not being allowed to express his devotion to Jesus would be like asking him to stop breathing. He simply cannot be quiet about his passion for God!

Devotion to Jesus is a conscious decision we must make. Jesus said, "No servant can serve two masters. Either he will hate the one and love the other, or he will be devoted to the one and despise the other" (Luke 16:13). If we are devoted to Jesus, everything else takes second place. Someone who is devoted to Jesus seeks to follow him in everything he does. "Everything to him was about Jesus," said Cindy.

Being devoted to Jesus means more than attending worship services, praying before meals or following the unwritten rules of our Christian tradition. It involves a heartfelt commitment to Jesus in everything we do. This is portrayed to others through our words, deeds, and treatment of others around us. Warren said, "His whole life was dedicated to Jesus." When we communicate our passion by expressing our devotion to Christ, we will stimulate others to know him.

A Passionate Discipler Is Enthusiastic

Unbelievers divulged that passionate disciplers are enthusiastic about communicating the joy they have as Jesus followers. One of the marks of enthusiasm was tone of voice. Amber said, "His tone of voice combined with his inviting personality resulted in his words coming across as passionate and persuasive." Terry agreed. "When he speaks, you can hear the passion in his voice. But he isn't condescending. He is able to show his passion, but he shows it in a loving way." It is daunting to realize that others make judgments on us based on our tone of voice. Nevertheless, it has been estimated that as much as 90 percent of communication is nonverbal, including tone of voice. This challenges us to be aware of the way we communicate with unbelievers. We need to exhibit passion in our speech, but in a way that is honest and heartfelt.

Disciplers also communicate enthusiasm about their love for God. "You can just tell that he gets into what he is talking about and that he loves God's Word," said Carol. "It was all he talked about!" Michael explained his discipler's passion this way. "My neighbor was so full of life, and talked about Jesus in such a 'passionate' way . . . and spoke of how he was leading her in life, and all the works he had done in her. To me, it made sense, I could see there was something different about her—a positive thing."

Being a disciple of Jesus is exciting! We have the greatest news in the universe! If we are in love with Jesus, our speech will naturally reflect passion for him. When we are enthusiastic about Jesus, others will sense our excitement and respond to his love. Enthusiasm for God is contagious!

A Passionate Discipler Is Driven

When I was growing up, my family spent Independence Day with other families on a large sandbar on the Tanana River. We spent the day eating lunch together, playing games, and—for those who dared—wading in the frigid river. At the peak of a warm summer, the temperature of the river sometimes reached forty-five degrees. When we first stepped out into the current, the icy waters made us involuntarily gasp. But we pushed on until our entire bodies turned brilliant red from the cold. Why did we do it? Because, in some strange way, it was entertaining! We were driven to endure the icy temperatures so we could have fun!

A discipler who is passionate is driven. This means that he is sincerely passionate about Jesus, and he expresses this through his actions. Being driven is the result of having an inner passion for Jesus. Samantha said, "Just talking to him you can tell he was always on fire for Jesus." A person who is driven naturally shares her joy with others. "He is not afraid to pour his heart and soul into his ministry," Brandon added.

We are called to share the good news of Jesus. However, if we lead lives that are viewed as irrelevant and boring to unbelievers, how can we expect to have any impact on them at all? This is not to say that any of us is perfect. We all struggle with sin. But unwittingly, as disciples of Jesus, we are often reluctant to passionately reveal through words and deeds that Jesus is the answer to all of life's difficulties. He has unfathomable power and strength that he wants to share with us! Others need to see that we are passionate about our walk with Jesus.

Not only do we need to express the passion in our lives to unbelievers, we also need to believe in the reason for our existence. If we are not passionate about Jesus, it will be evident to unbelievers. Making disciples happens when we are driven to seek and save others. It cannot happen by accident. Being intentional gives us the motivation and energy to disciple others.

Jesus has to be such a vibrant part of our lives that we cannot keep quiet about him and what he has done for us! We are often more passionate about sports, hobbies, and jobs than we are about making disciples. If we do not have passion as a follower of Christ, we need to reexamine our purposes for making disciples. Others need to see how our life has been changed by the transforming power of Jesus. When they understand our passion, they will be influenced to know the One who can light their path, shower them with love, and give meaning to their existence.

PASSION FOR DISCIPLING

I have a friend who has successfully climbed Alaska's Mount McKinley several times. Preparing for the ascent takes eight to ten months of difficult conditioning. No one exerts this much effort unless he is passionate about ascending the mountain. Making the actual climb is a strategic process that involves a team of people working together. The team hikes up 1,000 feet to bury food and supplies, and then hikes back down to camp for the night. The next day, the team hikes to the food and supplies, gathers it and ascends the next 1,000 feet. This process is repeated until the team establishes a camp at 17,000 feet. The last day involves ascending the final 3,000 feet to the summit.

Making disciples is much like climbing a mountain: it takes preparation, effort, and passion. New disciples of Jesus usually have a high degree of passion for sharing the gospel with others, but they may need assistance in facing the potential blizzards and frigid temperatures of making disciples. This is when others can step in and help us in our discipling efforts.

Those who have grown out of spiritual infancy and into the adolescent stage of faith may have lost some of the zeal found in new disciples of Jesus. If this describes us, climbing the mountain of discipleship may not have the novel appeal it once did, and the passion for making disciples needs to be reignited.

People who have encountered the mountain of discipleship many times have undoubtedly encountered many setbacks. They can either become cynical toward these experiences, or view them as potential opportunities for growth. It is not enough to say, "I have done my time" and retire our passion for discipling.

We often want to excuse ourselves from the call to make disciples. This is exactly what Moses did. When God called him to go to Pharaoh and ask him to free the Israelites, did Moses jump at the opportunity? No! He gave some pretty lame excuses for not serving God:

- "Who am I?" (Exod 3:11)
- "What shall I tell them?" (Exod 3:13)
- "What if they do not believe me or listen to me?" (Exod 4:1)
- "I am slow of speech and tongue." (Exod 4:10)

After God dispelled these excuses, Moses cried out in exasperation: "O Lord, please send someone else to do it" (Exod 4:13). God did not heed the excuses of Moses, because God had a task for him. Similarly, our excuses are hollow and meaningless to God, because he has a mission for us, and he expects us to be obedient to him.

What is your excuse? Perhaps you are fearful to share the good news with others because you do not have enough faith. Jesus wants to shine through you, but you are keeping him to yourself, locked away, chained to your doubts.

How we respond to the Great Commission is up to us. If we truly understand what it means to disciple others—we will not set our goals low—but will rise to the occasion and climb even higher! Anyone can be a discipler, but intentionality is expressed through a passionate desire to share the good news with others.

THE CHALLENGE OF BEING PASSIONATE

Luke emphasized the power of passion in his narrative of the rich man. The wealthy man died and went to hell. There, he was able to look and see his former servant Lazarus with Abraham. The rich man begged Abraham to cool his tongue with just a drop of water. Abraham refused. Read the rest of the story from Luke 16:27–31:

"He answered, 'Then I beg you, father, send Lazarus to my father's house, for I have five brothers. Let him warn them, so that they will not also come to this place of torment.' "Abraham replied, 'They have Moses and the Prophets; let them listen to them.' "'No, father Abraham,' he said, 'but if someone from the dead goes to them, they will repent.' "He said to him, 'If they do not listen to Moses and the Prophets, they will not be convinced even if someone rises from the dead.'"

The rich man was beside himself with grief over the possibility of his family ending up in hell. He passionately wanted to save his family—but it was too late. This is the same passion we need to have for our loved ones before it is too late for them.

The biggest hindrance to making disciples is not our lack of money or ability, but our lack of passion. Too often, Christians exert energy to form an impenetrable fortress from the rest of the world, instead of dangerously scouting for new unbelievers. Are you satisfied to maintain the status quo, or do you feel passionate enough to change the world?

QUESTIONS FOR DISCUSSION

- What are you most passionate about? Explain.

- Read Luke 13:31–35. What feelings do you think Jesus experienced in this passage?

- In what ways can we show unbelievers that we are devoted to God?

- Consider the excuses Moses gave to God. What excuses do we give for not discipling others?

- Read Luke 16:19–31. What lessons does this teach us today?

PERSONAL REFLECTION

- Where are you on the discipleship mountain? How can you climb even higher?

- Pray that God will incite within you a greater passion for unbelievers.

11

The Affiliative Model of Discipleship

Let's quit fiddling with religion
and do something to bring the world to Christ.

—BILLY SUNDAY

WHEN I BEGAN FOLLOWING Jesus, I was fortunate enough to be part of a church that taught people how to share the gospel with an unbelieving person. Unfortunately, the process of sharing the gospel was confined to learning a canned script, which began with a statement such as, "If you knew today was your last day to live, do you know for certain you would go to heaven?" If there were objections along the way, we were taught how to overcome them, point by point. The speech usually ended with something akin to, "Are you ready to accept Jesus as Lord of your life today?"

The primary difficulty with this approach to seeking unbelievers is that it was essentially a duplication of the traditional sales method. For many years, business schools and corporations have espoused a sales method that drives people to buy a particular product. To make a sale, it is necessary to follow explicit steps. The first step is to advertise the product. The goal is to make as many people as possible aware that the product exists. The next step is to make initial contact with people about the product. This is accomplished through cold calling, door knocking, or other similar method. Then, an appointment for a presentation is made. At the appointed time, the salesperson makes the scripted presentation, and handles any objections from the potential customer. He has been trained to handle these objections quickly and efficiently. When all questions are satisfactorily answered, the salesperson moves to close the sale. If the purchase is made, the salesperson asks the customer for people who may be interested in the product. There is frequently an incentive—such as free service for three months or fifty dollars off the next purchase—for each appointment with a referral. This method of selling has been used effectively for many years.

This traditional sales method has been nicknamed the "push" approach, because it requires the salesperson to use coercion—even manipulation—to persuade potential customers to buy the product. Often, pressure tactics are used, such as, "Available at this price today only." When I was younger, I encountered this teaching as I was being trained as a salesperson. Before I made my first presentation, my manager challenged me to tell the customer anything to make the sale. "Sometimes, you just have to be conniving," he said. The idea of intentionally deceiving someone to make a sale did not appeal to me, so I resigned from a potentially lucrative career in sales.

When we attempt to push others or coerce them in some way to follow Jesus, the purpose of making disciples is lost. The end does not justify the means. If we are seeking others to receive accolades from our church, we are no better than the salesperson that deceitfully makes sales to win a trip to Hawaii. Further, if our idea of making disciples is following a list of steps or reciting a canned script, we counteract the relationship factor in making disciples. Making disciples is a process of developing lasting relationships with people that will lead them to establish an eternal relationship with Jesus.

This chapter challenges us to think about the process of discipleship—why our traditional approach to the Great Commission does not work, and what we can do differently. A model for discipleship—based on lessons from the life of Jesus—is presented and explained. As we read this, it would be good to think about how we have discipled others, and what we can do to strengthen our calling.

THE SHOTGUN APPROACH

The greatest downfall of the push method of making disciples is that it uses a "shotgun approach" to reach customers. In other words, this approach attempts to hit everyone at once—like a ten-gauge shotgun discharges ammunition in an angle wide enough to hit everything in sight—without considering the individual needs of potential customers. Everyone is viewed as a potential customer. This technique expends unnecessary energy and money, and aims at customers who have not yet realized a need for the product.

Some years ago, my church decided to host a citywide gospel meeting. To promote the campaign, we organized a plan to knock on the door of every household in that city. Volunteers from neighboring churches and a Christian college came to help. We rented the largest auditorium in town for the big event. After knocking on nearly 10,000 doors and advertising the meeting with posters and radio spots, guess how many people came to our meeting? Not one. After recovering from the disappointment, we realized that the "shotgun approach" was not the best method to use.

Churches today still use this approach to spread the gospel message. These churches try to offer something for everyone by providing a full spectrum of classes, activities, and services: muscle car ministries, quilting clubs, aerobic exercise classes and the like—hoping that they will eventually hit upon a spiritual need. We convince ourselves that we are on the right track because we are working so hard. When the body of Christ is run like a social club, we inadvertently present a watered-down version of the cross. We may have some success in the beginning, but ultimately this tactic falls short of the mark.

Jesus described the problem with the shotgun method in the parable of the sower, as told in Luke 8:5–8: "A farmer went out to sow his seeds. As he was scattering the seed, some fell along the path; it was trampled on, and the birds of the air ate it up. Some fell on rock, and when it came up, the plants withered because they had no moisture. Other seed fell among thorns, which grew up with it and choked the plants. Still other seed fell on good soil. It came up and yielded a crop, a hundred times more than was sown."

When we use the shotgun approach to find unbelievers to disciple, we are like the farmer in the parable who scattered his seeds everywhere. Much of the effort we generate will fall on the deaf ears of those who are along the path, on the rock, or among the thorns, and the message will not grow roots and produce fruit. This technique does not intentionally seek people who have the spiritual nutrients of good soil.

Another difficulty with the shotgun approach to making disciples is that it does not consider the dignity of people. No one wants to be considered a "prospect" or a potential sale to close. People today have grown suspicious and skeptical from shady telemarketers and aggressive door-to-door salesmen. When we treat unbelievers as a means of adding jewels to our heavenly crown, we are no better than a devious used car salesman who views potential customers as dollar signs. Viewing someone merely as a contact to join our exclusive church society minimizes the nurturing essence of making disciples. If this is the motivation we have for telling others about Jesus, they will be able to sniff out our insincerity in a heartbeat. Regrettably, many people have been left with a bad taste in their mouths from well-meaning disciples of Jesus.

THE TARGET APPROACH

A better tactic to use in seeking others is the "target approach." This means that we thoughtfully and prayerfully aim to reach and disciple those who have unmet spiritual needs. When Jesus called his first apostles, he did not take out an ad in the Jerusalem Times. He walked directly to Peter and Andrew and asked them to follow him (Matt 4:19). Like Jesus, we need to target people who are spiritually hungry. They are the "good soil" that he called us to disciple. When we scatter spiritual seed among these people, Jesus will produce a harvest within them that is a hundred times more fruitful. If we want to be intentional disciplers, we need to focus our energy, time, and money on people who have deep spiritual cravings.

RELATIONSHIP IS CRUCIAL

As the research has shown, the majority of unbelievers who gave their lives to Jesus were influenced by an intimate relationship with another person. This is in stark contrast to traditional evangelistic methods which do not consider relationship as integral to conversion.

The importance of relationships in making disciples was made apparent to me a couple of years ago. Our church was planning to have a picnic in a neighborhood park and decided to personally canvass all the homes in that neighborhood. As we were handing out flyers to people, one of our church members struck up a conversation with a woman. As he described what our church had planned for the day, her eyes lit up and she replied that she would love to come. That is, until she looked down and noticed the stack of flyers in his hands. When she saw that, her whole face fell as she realized that he was not only inviting her, but the whole neighborhood. She ended up not coming to the picnic. Can you blame her? In all probability, she no longer felt special or important.

The reason mass marketing and canvassing are ineffective marketing strategies is because they lack the foundation of relationship. These methods invade a person's privacy, and only succeed at building brick walls of resistance around potential disciples. A relationship is especially critical when unbelievers need to entrust someone with their personal soul concerns.

A PARADIGM SHIFT

Einstein said that the definition of insanity was "Doing the same thing over and over again and expecting different results." We have learned the hard way that the traditional push model no longer works—for sales or for sharing the good news. People on the cutting edge of business marketing are now waking up to this realization. As a result, the business world is now on the horizon of a major paradigm shift in sales training. Not surprisingly, the new paradigm emphasizes relationships. It is usually coined the Attraction Model of Sales.

The Attraction Model of Sales is not a list of techniques. It focuses on identifying and satisfying personal needs within people out of a genuine concern for them. As the relationship is being built, the salesperson gathers further information about the needs of the prospect, and formulates a solution to offer the prospect. The offer is given in a genuine gesture of concern. If a relationship of mutual trust has been established, there will be no need for either party to act defensively. The end result is the creation of a relationship that has a long-term value for both parties.

THE AFFILIATIVE MODEL

It is possible to translate the principles of the Attraction Model and apply its foundational structure to the process of making disciples. We propose that this process be called the Affiliative Model of Discipleship. The word "affiliative" is used instead of "attraction," because of the relationship factor in making disciples. Moreover, the phrase "Attraction Model" has been used recently in Christian circles to describe the shotgun approach of seeking others with the gospel. The Affiliative Model does not do that. It assumes that the process of making disciples is built on trust and mutual respect.

The Affiliative Model is not a step-by-step formula for making disciples, but a process of understanding the spiritual evolution of unbelievers. Discipling others to follow Jesus is a fluid process that is guided by the Holy Spirit. Reducing the process to a series of steps naively binds the function and will of the Spirit. Regardless of our efforts, God will not be boxed in; he is bigger and more powerful than we can imagine! The Affiliative Model should not be considered a panacea to making disciples; rather, it should be regarded as a means of shaping the way we relationally guide others to know Jesus.

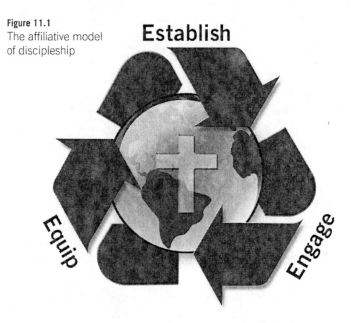

Figure 11.1
The affiliative model of discipleship

Figure 11.1 illustrates the Affiliative Model for sharing the gospel with others. This model graphically exemplifies discipleship as a process that involves intentionally establishing relationships with unbelievers, engaging them in spiritual dialogue which ultimately leads to their conversion, and equipping them to make disciples of others. Also observe that the model demonstrates discipleship as a continuous, dynamic process which, when put into practice, becomes recycled. It is a never-ending task that extends to all future generations.

As designated by this model, Jesus is necessarily at the center of discipleship. We cannot lead others to Jesus unless we are first following him. Modeling Jesus is at the quintessential core of discipleship. When we demonstrate the character of Jesus to others, we will lead unbelievers into relationship with him. Of course, discipling is much more than an exhibition; Christlikeness emanates from us when we have been transformed into the image of Jesus. Emulating Jesus is not merely something we do; it is a lifestyle.

Modeling Jesus needs to be the overarching theme of our lives. The apostle Paul put it this way: "I want to know Christ and the power of his resurrection and the fellowship of sharing in his sufferings, becoming like him in his death, and so, somehow, to attain to the resurrection from the dead" (Phil 3:10–11). Being like Jesus needs to consume our thoughts and drive our actions to the point that we actually become conformed into his image.

Sometimes, people may be so far from Jesus they can't see him at all, but if we dangerously model Jesus they can see him in us. When we are not afraid to imitate Jesus in our lives, unbelievers will come to know him. This is how modeling Jesus has such a powerful impact on others, and why it is crucial in the discipling process.

Establish Relationship

The first component in the Affiliative Model is to establish a relationship with an unbeliever. Obviously, it is not possible to disciple someone unless we are first in relationship with her. Although Jesus touched the lives of many people in his ministry, he did not develop long-term relationships with all of them. He did not have the time to personally disciple hundreds of people. Instead, he chose twelve men with whom he intimately worked. Mark 3:14 said, "He appointed twelve—designating them apostles—that they might be with him and that he might send them out to preach." Jesus discipled these men as they traveled together. Of these men, he hand-picked three—Peter, James, and John—with whom he developed especially close relationships. He entrusted them to see him transfigured with Moses and Elijah, and he wanted them to be close to him as he prayed in the garden of Gethsemane.

One of the biggest obstacles standing in the way of making disciples is not actively seeking to establish relationships with unbelievers. For a variety of reasons—fear of rejection, contentment with our lives, or reluctance to invest in the spiritual lives of others—we have refused to initiate relationships with unbelievers. Many of us are content to stay within the confines of our little worlds. We spend most of our time interacting with our Christian friends. We perpetuate the idea that the church is nothing more than some elitist club by filling our calendars with potlucks, camping trips, and parties for every occasion. We often implement ministries that perpetuate relationships with other members. We even design worship services that are focused on satisfying our own desires. Living within the church walls discourages many potential opportunities for making disciples, because everyone we know already follows Jesus. We have these affiliations down pat; unfortunately, if we limit our interactions to other disciples, we naively close the doors to unbelievers who need Jesus.

It is quite interesting to note at this point that the research found a direct correlation between the ages of the disciple and the discipler who influenced them. Except in the case of the youngest disciples in the research study, those age thirteen or younger, all age groups were most influenced by people within their same age bracket.

Figure 11.2
Influence of discipler based on age

Age of Unbeliever

	13 & under	14–28	29–43	44–62
14–28	15%	**38%**	22%	18%
29–43	**61%**	32%	**56%**	2%
44–62	21%	24%	21%	**61%**
63+	3%	6%	1%	19%

(Left axis label: **Age of Discipler**)

As figure 11.2 indicates, 38 percent of unbelievers who were between fourteen and twenty-eight years old were influenced by disciplers who were the same age. For unbelievers who were between twenty-nine and forty-three years old, 56 percent were influenced most by disciplers within their age group; and for people who were between forty-four and sixty-two years old, 60 percent were influenced by disciplers in their same age group.

We can infer from these results that we have the most influence on people who are around our own age. This does not mean we cannot have an impact on people outside of our age group; rather, we have a greater influence on people who are in our age bracket. Knowing this will help us pay special attention to unbelieving people in our age group, while not discounting others. Once again, this demonstrates the value of taking the target approach.

Why were unbelievers who were thirteen or younger not influenced by people their own age? At first glance, this may not seem like a significant finding. However, notice that—not only were these disciples not influenced by people in their own age group—they were not even appreciably impacted by those who were between fourteen and twenty-eight years old. Disciplers that had the most influence on unbelievers who were thirteen years old and younger were between the ages of twenty-nine and forty-three—two age brackets higher than unbelievers. One plausible interpretation may be that most relatives of unbelievers were in the twenty-nine to forty-three year old age group. Another contributing factor may be that this age group of disciplers consisted of a large percentage of ministers. We may reasonably infer from these data that youth ministers who are at least one generation removed from youth will likely have the greatest impact on them. Churches that typically employ very young youth ministers may need to rethink their hiring strategies and intentionally seek more seasoned youth ministers.

Additionally, as previous research has revealed, 80 percent of unbelievers gave their lives to Jesus before they were twenty-five years old. Of these, the majority give their lives to him at age eighteen or younger.[1] The large percentage of people who are converted at a young age reveals the importance of targeting young people who have spiritual needs. This is not to say that we should ignore those who are older—because we can certainly have an influence on them. Rather, it shows that we need to recognize the available resources we have, such as youth ministers, and use them to the fullest.

Establishing relationships is not rocket science. The difficulty comes with viewing others as potential disciples. It is possible to have many superficial relationships, but it is quite another matter to cultivate deeper relationships with some of them. We will not make disciples unless we, like

---

1. Barna. *The Habits of Highly Effective Churches*, 120. This was also confirmed by our research.

Jesus, carefully select individuals to disciple and intentionally strengthen relationships with them. This will develop mutual trust and thereby provide opportunities for leading people to Jesus.

Engage in Spiritual Dialogue

Engaging in spiritual dialogue is another component in the Affiliative Model. A relationship built on trust and respect is conducive to meaningful, open dialogue. The purpose of engaging in spiritual dialogue with others is to lead them to Jesus. This is accomplished by guiding others to personally know the grace, power, and love that only he provides.

The research revealed that unbelievers were most likely to be led to conversion when disciplers initiated spiritual discussions with them. As disciplers, it is our responsibility to initiate these discussions. When a genuine and mutually trusting relationship has been established, disciplers who initiate dialogue are not considered to be pushy or coercive. On the contrary, as shown in the research, when Jesus is introduced in the context of this kind of relationship, it is interpreted by unbelievers as an expression of sincerity and care for them. If we are modeling Jesus in our lives, it may be that an unbeliever is waiting for us to make the first move.

Another aspect of spiritual dialogue is expressing our faith to others. Jesus told his disciples in Acts 1:8, "you will be my witnesses in Jerusalem, and in all Judea and Samaria, and to the ends of the earth." Being a witness to others is not something we do, it is something we are. Everyone has struggles and difficulties in life. People who depend on their own abilities do not know God, but people who are in relationship with him are empowered with strength, wisdom, and faith. We need to show others that God carries us through the tough times. He will never give up on us, and he will certainly never leave us. This is the God we can help others know!

Articulating our faith with unbelievers naturally spurs them to ask questions about our spiritual walk. In the affiliative process, if a trusting relationship has been established, these questions will be asked out of clarification and sincerity, not as an invitation to debate.

Through the leading of the Holy Spirit, spiritual discussions eventually lead others to accept or reject Jesus. There are no guarantees in making disciples, and there are no miraculous words we can say in conversations with others. Just as an electrical conduit routes energy from one source to another, we are conduits through which the Holy Spirit speaks to unbelievers. In John 16:13, Jesus said, "But when he, the Spirit of truth, comes, he will guide you into all truth. He will not speak on his own; he will speak only what he hears, and he will tell you what is yet to come." It is assuring to know that God is leading the discipling relationship! Unbelievers will come to Jesus when they are compelled to commit their lives to him.

Baptism is also a critical component of the discipling process. Baptism is the most intimate part of becoming like Jesus. Paul explains how this happens in Romans 6:3–5: "Or don't you know that all of us who were baptized into Christ Jesus were baptized into his death? We were therefore buried with him through baptism into death in order that, just as Christ was raised from the dead through the glory of the Father, we too may live a new life. If we have been united with him like this in his death, we will certainly also be united with him in his resurrection."

This passage beautifully illustrates how baptism is an emulation of Christ. When we are immersed through baptism, we are imitating the death of Jesus in the tomb; and, when we are raised out of our watery graves, we are replicating how Jesus was raised from his grave. As a result, we both have new lives! Galatians 3:27 NLT puts it like this: "And all who have been united with Christ in baptism have put on Christ, like putting on new clothes." This passage makes it clear that we are baptized into Christ, not into a church. Additionally, when we are baptized, we are actually putting Jesus on like a protective garment! Imagine having the opportunity to explain this to someone! Baptism should always be part of the discipling process.

Making disciples out of unbelievers takes time. As shown in chapter three, after spiritual dialogue was initiated with unbelievers, the average length of time it took until they chose to follow him was more than a year. Knowing this helps us understand the commitment level required for making disciples. We need to be prepared to devote ourselves to long-term discipling relationships. We must have the patience and endurance necessary to intimately share our lives with others, knowing they may or may not follow Jesus. If we want to intentionally make disciples, we need to make the conscious decision to devote much of our time investing in relationships with unbelievers.

Equip People to Disciple Others

The third component of the Affiliative Model is equipping people to disciple others. The Great Commission does not end with conversion—Jesus makes it clear that the role of teaching must continue. Jesus commands us to teach others to obey everything he has commanded us (Matthew 28:20). When an unbeliever gives her life to Jesus we should rejoice, but our work is unfinished. The Great Commission involves teaching a new believer how to be spiritually mature and equipping her to repeat the discipling process with others. If we neglect to teach her these things, she will be spiritually handicapped.

If new disciples of Christ are left at the starting gates with no fuel to run the spiritual race, they will suffer spiritual stagnation and not get very far. As disciplers, we need to make sure that this does not happen to newborn followers of Jesus. They need spiritual tools—not only to disciple others—but also to adequately grow in their faith.

The Affiliative approach to discipleship is a never-ending endeavor. When someone commits his life to Jesus, the cycle begins all over again— he is called to go and disciple someone else. In others words, making disciples is a process of recycling the process of discipleship. If we fail to help others grow spiritually and equip them to disciple others, they will not be able to lead lives that are entirely committed to Jesus.

USING THE AFFILIATIVE MODEL

Although the principles of the Affiliative Model have been referred to as components, they are not necessarily incremental. In other words, the order does not matter as much as the action. It may be that someone asks you about Jesus before you have established a relationship with him. If that is the case, by all means—answer him! Another scenario may be that someone has been watching you from a distance. You might be the person who always gives a cheerful greeting to the person who serves you coffee or tea. No matter what kind of day the person has had, he can count on you to make it a little better. Because of your positive spirit, one day this person decides to open up to you about a difficulty he is going through. That may give you an opportunity to engage in spiritual dialogue.

Sometimes the principles in the Affiliative Model occur simultaneously; we are doing two or three things at once. Jesus did whatever it took to share the good news with people. We may be developing a relationship with someone and concurrently sharing Jesus with them. We may be starting to equip someone at the same time we are engaging in spiritual dialogue with him. There is no miracle formula for discipleship. The central thing to remember is that God wants to use us to disciple others.

Understanding discipleship is easy: we model Jesus in everything we do. This affects how we establish relationships with unbelievers, the ways we engage in spiritual conversations with them, and how we equip them to continue the process. Discipleship is quite difficult from a practicality standpoint, because it is human nature to want to see measurable results for our efforts. It takes personal effort, but it also requires us to have an inordinate amount of trust in God.

Spiritual growth is a mysterious process; it does not happen automatically. The apostle Paul acknowledged this in 1 Corinthians 3:6: "I planted the seed, Apollos watered it, but God made it grow." We can plant and water, but only God gives the growth. We are in the seed-planting business. We may not know if or when a seed of faith we planted in someone will take root, grow, and produce fruit of faithfulness. Nevertheless, we are called to spread the good news of Jesus Christ to others.

THE CHALLENGE OF DISCIPLING

Who do you know who has spiritual needs? Do not expect your church to reach her; do not wait for your minister to visit her. It is your responsibility to plant the seed of faith in her. You may be the only one standing between her and Jesus!

Are you frightened at the thought of finding an unbeliever with whom you can initiate a discipling relationship? If so, why? Are you fearful that others may reject you at the first mention of Jesus? Are you concerned that you will not have the right words to say? It is time to put your trust in God. He will not leave you stranded because he has chosen to be in relationship with you, and he will never forsake you. God will bless you as you disciple others. He will give you wisdom when you are at a loss for words, he will give you strength when you are discouraged, and he will provide guidance when your discipling paths take you to dead ends. God will help you live dangerously! This chapter offered a skeleton model for making disciples. The next chapter will discuss ways to put flesh on this model and intentionally disciple others.

QUESTIONS FOR DISCUSSION

- Have you ever been a door-to-door salesperson? Describe your experience.

- Why is establishing relationships with unbelievers better than the traditional push approach?

- Read Luke 8:5–15. Why is it not good to scatter seeds of discipleship everywhere? What are some ways we can intentionally target unbelievers?

- Read Romans 6:3–8. In what ways is baptism an emulation of Jesus?

- Read 1 Corinthians 3:6. Is this passage reassuring? How?

PERSONAL REFLECTION

- Are you intentionally trying to establish and cultivate relationships with unbelievers? If not, how can you begin doing this?

- Ask God to show you people who have spiritual needs.

12

How to Live Dangerously

Some want to live within the sound of church or chapel bell;
I want to run a rescue shop within a yard of hell.

—C. T. Studd

WHAT IS IT LIKE to go home? Recently, I had the opportunity to visit my hometown after being gone for many years. It seemed funny to me that people seemed to remember me the way I used to be. "Shawn, you keep getting taller." "Shawn, you're not skinny anymore." "Shawn, is that gray hair I see?" It's understandable. I don't look the same. However, many people who saw me grow up still think of me as that little, red-haired preacher's kid. They actually seem surprised that I'm physically mature.

I can imagine what was going through people's minds when Jesus entered his hometown. When he went to Nazareth and began to teach in the synagogue, people were surprised and said, "'Where did this man get these things?' they asked. 'What's this wisdom that has been given him, that he even does miracles! Isn't this the carpenter? Isn't this Mary's son and the brother of James, Joseph, Judas and Simon? Aren't his sisters here with us?' And they took offense at him" (Mark 6:2–3).

People remembered Jesus as a child. He was the son of God, but to people in his hometown, he was just Jesus, son of Joseph the carpenter. They knew his parents, brothers, and sisters. People who watched Jesus grow up thought of him no more highly than any other boy from Nazareth. They had seen him play with the other children, they watched him learn carpentry, and they knew that he had little, if any, formal education. Jesus did not stand out in a crowd. Isaiah prophesied about Jesus when he said, "He had no beauty or majesty to attract us to him, nothing in his appearance that we should desire him" (Isa 53:2). Now, this same, ordinary Jesus that everyone knew was preaching and performing miracles!

Just as people in my hometown were astonished at my adult stature, the citizens of Nazareth were shocked to see Jesus' spiritual growth. It was just too much for them to handle. This caused Jesus to respond in Mark 6:4, "Only in his hometown, among his relatives and in his own house is a prophet without honor."

Since Jesus did not command the respect of his own townspeople, it is all the more extraordinary that he was able to accomplish so much during his short lifetime. How did he do it? He lived dangerously by intentionally discipling others! This chapter will discuss how to make disciples by living like Jesus. We cannot be Jesus, but when are transformed into his image, we can reflect his traits, his actions, and his mission.

ESTABLISH RELATIONSHIPS

Making disciples is not possible without establishing intimate relationships with people. This is not to imply that we cannot or should not have an influence on a large group of people; rather, we need to target people with whom we can develop intimate relationships. Like Jesus, we need to intentionally establish relationships with people outside the church walls who are hurting, confused, and broken. Where do we find people who need Jesus? Anywhere! We simply need to open our eyes to the possibilities. One way to do this is by looking for opportunities to build rapport with people in our everyday routines. My wife and I have made it a habit to ask servers permission to address people by their first names. They always respond in the affirmative. In fact, they are usually very pleasantly surprised that we have taken time to notice them beyond someone who refills our iced teas. We can do the same thing in places we frequent, such as grocery stores, hair salons, or banks. One of the most evangelistic people I know is a young mother who develops relationships naturally with other mothers she meets at parks or the local preschoolers club. Then she takes time to get to know them and their needs. Every day we come into contact with people who are spiritually hungry and need Jesus.

Go to Unbelievers

How did Jesus intentionally seek unbelievers? He went to them! Likewise, if we desire to establish relationships with unbelievers, we need to intentionally pursue them. We have had a fortress mentality for too long. We cannot establish relationships with unbelievers if we continue to separate ourselves from them. We need to take Jesus' approach to being in the world but not of the world—which means accepting unbelievers for who they are—while holding on to our own faith. Instead of being repelled by those outside our church, we need to engage our communities. This involves going to places they go, reading the books they read, and watching the movies they watch.

Intentionally engaging in culture does not mean we should become like the world or accept values that conflict with biblical principles. This demands us to have pure hearts and clean consciences as we seek to establish relationships with unbelievers. We are called to be salt and light to the world (Matt 5:13–14). Instead of letting culture influence us, we need to impact the world with the love of Jesus.

Seek the Spiritually Needy

Matthew 10:5–6 records what Jesus told his disciples when he sent them into the world: "These twelve Jesus sent out with the following instructions: 'Do not go among the Gentiles or enter any town of the Samaritans. *Go rather to the lost sheep of Israel*'" [my emphasis]. Specifically, we need to establish relationships with people who are searching for meaning in their lives—people who are aching for spiritual significance.

Since research has shown that the majority of people come to know Jesus before the age of twenty-five, we also need to pay special attention to young unbelievers with whom we can initiate relationships. One way to do this is by volunteering in local middle schools and high schools—especially if we have children in those schools. We can be advisors to clubs, chaperone dances or trips, and organize fund-raising events. If we know students who are already following Jesus, it would be quite natural to pray with those students about their unbelieving friends. The idea is to initiate relationships with young people who have spiritual needs.

Expand Our Horizons

If our relationship potential with others is bound by our current lifestyles, it is time to expand our relationship horizons. It could be that we are neglecting the needs of others. What are your interests? Become involved in activities you enjoy, with the distinct purpose of meeting others in places like health clubs, community sporting clubs, and parent clubs.

Volunteer at hospitals, rest homes, or at community events such as car shows, parades, or charity events. These activities bring people together, and provide opportunities for establishing relationships.

If you are a minister, arrange your schedule to spend less time in the church office so that you will have more time to become more integrally involved in the life of your community. Ministers often spend too much time maintaining relationships with people in churches instead of forging new ground with those in the community. Until we break out of our limited social world, we may never be aware of people who need the rest that Jesus so tenderly provides.

Maintain Genuine Motives

Relationships must be developed out of genuine motives. Our ultimate goal is leading people to Jesus, but we need to look for needs and develop relationships with people because they are fellow children of God. Some people may never want to be found. That should not hinder us from opening our lives to them. A relationship with another person should never be contingent upon her eventual acceptance of Jesus. The process of discipling others does not have strings attached. Jesus shared his love with many who did not follow him. Remember that we are in the seed-planting business, and we may never know the impact we have on another person. Our mandate is to spread the love of God with everyone—whether or not it leads to conversion.

Serve Others

Part of identifying the needs in unbelievers is looking for ways to serve them. Jesus identified people with needs and humbly served them. He said in Mark 10:45, "For even the Son of Man did not come to be served, but to serve, and to give his life as a ransom for many." Who do we know that could benefit from being served, and how can we serve them? My wife constantly impresses me with her ability to find opportunities to serve others. When friends of ours have a new baby, my wife cooks them a meal and brings it to them; when she discovers that young couples are unable to go on dates because they have small children, she offers to babysit; and when she finds people that need help moving, she offers my assistance! There are people all around us who are in need of our help—we simply need to find those needs and fulfill them through service.

Serving others is not always convenient. In Matthew 5:41, Jesus said, "If someone forces you to go one mile, go with him two miles." People do not expect others to be giving. We can pleasantly surprise them by going the extra mile. When we do this, relationships will be built, thus leading people to Jesus.

If we choose not to serve unbelievers, we could be missing out on many relationship opportunities. We should be looking for ways to serve unbelievers, regardless of whether or not we enter into discipling relationships with them.

Initiate Service through Your Church

After years of being inwardly focused, churches are beginning to understand the value of reaching out to communities by serving them. A prominent church in southern California decided to serve its community by investigating the possibility of building a rescue mission, an after-school tutoring program for at-risk children, and an employment training program. I was called as a consultant by this church to help research the feasibility of launching these projects. This church now serves people in its community with these needs and brings Jesus to them through relationships with church members.

As members of local churches, we can influence our church leadership to look for ways to serve our community. We can offer to organize meals to feed the hungry in our community; gather clothes from our members to give to people in need; or we can get permission to turn part of our church property into a garden, so people in our community can plant and cultivate their own vegetables.

We can probably think of many more ways to serve that fit our unique church and community. It is the mission of both churches and individuals to serve others. This will lead to opportunities for making disciples.

ENGAGE IN SPIRITUAL DIALOGUE

Once a trusting relationship has been firmly established with someone, it is time to engage in spiritual dialogue with him. How long should we wait to engage in spiritual dialogue? If we examine how Jesus discipled others, we will find that he often did not wait to begin spiritual discussions with others. For example, when Jesus encountered the woman at Jacob's well, he initiated spiritual conversation in response to the woman's question.

There are two main applications we can draw from this incident. First, by segueing from well water to living water, Jesus opened the door for discussion about eternal life. Second, Jesus initiated spiritual conversation with the woman almost immediately.

Chapter three revealed that almost half of unbelievers were influenced to give their lives to Jesus when disciplers initiated spiritual dialogue after knowing the unbelievers three months or less. Figure 12.1 indicates that when relatives were filtered out of this correlation, 63 percent of unbelievers committed their lives to Jesus when disciplers initiated spiritual dialogue within three months.

Figure 12.1
How long did you know this person before Jesus came up in conversation?
(filtered without relatives)

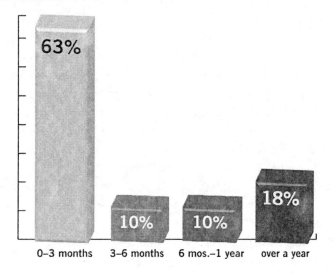

| 0–3 months | 3–6 months | 6 mos.–1 year | over a year |

This is logical, since relatives probably knew each other more than a year before Jesus was brought up. This also suggests that disciplers who are not relatives are more likely to initiate spiritual discussions sooner. As disciplers, we need to intentionally initiate spiritual discussions with others; and, to be most effective, it is better if we begin these conversations early in the relationship. How early depends on a myriad of factors: the depth of the relationship, the receptiveness of the unbeliever, and our level of passion for sharing the gospel.

Introducing Jesus into a relationship should also be offered out of a genuine concern for the unbeliever. If people we know have concerns about a particular problem and share it with us, it would be quite easy to ask them if they have prayed about it. Depending upon the depth of the relationship, we could even ask the person for permission to pray for him. You can surely think of many more ways to initiate dialogue about Jesus. Initiating spiritual dialogue is a dangerous thing to do; it takes boldness and entails risk, but it has eternal consequences!

Maintain a Spirit of Humility

Unbelievers who were led to Jesus through a discipling relationship were asked, "Why did you feel comfortable discussing spiritual matters with this person?" They indicated that they were comfortable engaging in spiritual discussions with someone who demonstrates humility. This requires us to have gentle attitudes. Kimberly said, "I think it took less than a year. She was very gentle and didn't push anything." Similarly, Kevin said, "He acted like my opinion mattered to him, and he didn't try to force his opinions and beliefs on me."

Being pushy or pressuring people to come to Jesus does not encourage spiritual discussion. As disciplers, the last thing we want to do is push anyone to follow Jesus or pressure her in any way. This kind of relationship does not benefit us or unbelievers. If we have humble hearts, engaging in spiritual dialogue will not threaten them. Ellen said, "It was a nonthreatening situation—no pamphlets, no 'come to Jesus' talk—just friendship and discussion."

A spirit of humility breaks down the barriers of resistance and opens the doors for spiritual dialogue. Brett said, "There was no pressure. Since we were friends, I admired him and it was easier to talk about."

Our job is not to give others a "spiritual sales pitch," but to facilitate and encourage their faith development. We need to make discipling as enjoyable as possible by aspiring to develop a positive—even fun—environment. The challenge of initiating spiritual discussions is to be nonthreatening by letting Jesus shine through us in all our relationships. If we let him guide us, he can effectively use us to disciple others.

The way we initiate spiritual dialogue is critical to the conversion process. In this case, first impressions make a difference. A question such as, "Do you know if you are saved?" may be asked out of sincerity, but may be considered offensive or even insulting to the unbelieving person. Spiritual conversation should be a natural extension of our relationships. For example, a new friend of mine recently lost his job. He felt depressed and beaten. As we talked, I casually offered, "God has the perfect job just waiting for you." He looked down for a moment, then looked back at me with moist eyes and replied, "Thank you." I took a risk by even suggesting such a thing, but my friend responded, and we now have regular spiritual discussions.

Watch Your Language

We also need to be careful not to disenfranchise people in our spiritual discussions by the words we use. Oftentimes, we use "Christianese" so naturally we forget that others may not understand us. Examples of Christianese are: Holy Spirit, testimony, witness, assurance, redemption, resurrection, confession, and justification. If someone did not grow up going to church, "Here I raise my Ebenezer" and "Jehovah Jireh" make about as much sense as "triple net lease" and "current ratio" do to a person outside the financial industry. If we want our spiritual discussions with others to be effective, we need to speak their language. This requires us to break out of our comfortable Christian shells and relate to unbelievers using non-churchy words.

Submit to the Holy Spirit

The goal of engaging in spiritual discussions with unbelievers is to eventually lead them to conversion. However, our role in the discipling process is first and foremost to willfully submit ourselves to the Holy Spirit's leading. The apostle Paul said, "Since we live by the Spirit, let us keep in step with the Spirit (Galatians 5:25). His methods will likely not be ours; his timing may not be ours—but we need to trust the Spirit's guidance.

I learned a lesson about following the Spirit's leading a few years ago. After investing eight months of weekly studies with a woman, she told me that she had decided to follow Jesus! However, my excitement soon dissipated when she canceled all future studies with me. Soon after, she moved away. I later discovered that her unbelieving husband became angry when she told him her decision, and actually forbid her to continue her studies. Unbelievers may or may not come to know Jesus, but this should not diminish our discipling efforts or our trust in God's wisdom.

Engage in Spiritual Dialogue through Small Groups

Many people or faith communities have small groups that meet in homes. If we are involved in a small group, we can invite our unbelieving friends to come with us. They can meet other disciples of Jesus, and engage in spiritual conversations with a community of believers. A group that meets in a home is less threatening than meeting in a church building, and it is a relaxing and natural way to talk about spiritual matters.

If we want to use small groups to engage in spiritual dialogue with unbelievers, the members of our group need to be accepting of unbelievers and prepared to respond to their questions and comments in a non-judgmental fashion. This will likely involve training group members about their vital roles in discipling others, and how they can utilize spiritual conversations as an integral part of that process.

Baptize

If unbelievers decide to follow Jesus, we have reason to celebrate! But we cannot forget that baptism is an integral part of the Great Commission. Discipleship includes emulating the death, burial, and resurrection of Jesus Christ through baptism. Baptism means that we are symbolically immersed into the blood of Jesus, which completely engulfs us and permeates our soul. When unbelievers are ready to lead dangerous lives, they will need to take this step.

EQUIP OTHERS SPIRITUALLY THROUGH TEACHING

Following Jesus is the beginning of the Christian walk. If we want to be truly intentional about discipling others, we need to continue the process. Equipping others typically begins at their conversion. However, it is not necessarily distinct from establishing relationships and engaging in spiritual dialogue. Equipping can begin early in the discipling relationship. For instance, if someone begins attending a small group Bible study with us and she desires to invite a friend to the study, she may ask us advice on the best way to approach her friend. Our response involves equipping her, regardless if she has committed her life to Jesus.

Equipping begins with us modeling the discipleship process to an unbeliever, but it continues throughout the relationship. As we follow the ways Jesus discipled others, people will come to understand and appreciate discipling through their experiences with us. In turn, they will develop the knowledge and skills necessary to repeat the process with others. One of our main objectives is to teach intentional discipleship as a continuous, cyclical process.

The Role of the Church in Equipping

Although our role in discipleship extends to equipping newborn believers, churches can also play a vital role in this process. Paul instructed the first-century church in Ephesians 4:11–12 NLT: "Now these are the gifts Christ gave to the church: the apostles, the prophets, the evangelists, and the pastors and teachers. Their responsibility is to equip God's people to do his work and build up the church, the body of Christ." Leaders in the church are the ones Paul designated as being primarily responsible for preparing, or equipping people for building up the body of Christ.

At this point of a disciple's spiritual life, she is likely to be involved in a local church. Thus, she will be influenced by a community of believers. A church can be a spiritual training center for disciples. If our churches do not formally equip new disciples, we, as passionate members of our local congregations, need to influence our leadership to begin the process of equipping. Churches can help equip people by offering to train believers for the mission of making disciples.

There is no specific system or series of steps in equipping. How we equip others depends upon our relationship with them and their individual needs. Nevertheless, there are some universal principles that can be followed in any equipping relationship. We can equip others by guiding them to develop an intimate relationship with Jesus, increase their knowledge, and teach them how to disciple others.

Help Develop Intimacy with Jesus

Since discipleship is built upon relationships with people, the primary concern in equipping is to help others build an intimate relationship with Jesus. This is crucial in strengthening their own faith and in their discipling relationships with others. Teaching intimacy with Jesus begins with us demonstrating the relationship we have with him. Our definitive goal is to lead others into a committed relationship with Jesus, but they will learn how to do that by watching our example. Others will scrutinize every aspect of our relationship with Jesus, and will emulate it. This is why it is so critical to develop an intimate relationship with our Lord before we begin discipling unbelievers. We can also help others nurture their relationship with Jesus by teaching them to understand and apply spiritual disciplines in their lives.

When people develop an intimacy with Jesus, they will become transformed into his image. This means that they will internalize the traits of Jesus, and will be equipped to disciple others by being like him.

Increase Knowledge

Equipping others is a process of guiding others to deliberately increase their knowledge of God's Word. Consistent attention to Bible study is the best way of allowing God's words to permeate our minds and hearts. If we want to continue the cycle of discipleship, we need to teach others to have a solid biblical foundation. They need to be able to repeat the process with other disciples. Part of our role in helping disciples increase their knowledge is teaching them how to study the Bible. We need to teach what we have learned about biblical interpretation, and offer practical ways that they can apply biblical principles in their lives.

Teach the Discipleship Process

Through the discipling relationship, unbelievers are with us on a spiritual journey, and they need us to continue guiding them after they have given their lives to Jesus. Equipping is a lifelong process, because we are always growing in the faith. People I discipled many years ago still call me for spiritual advice. We need to be spiritually prepared to stick with the people we lead to Jesus.

Teaching the discipleship process also involves studying how Jesus discipled others: how he approached people, what he said to them, his attitude toward others, and his passion for discipleship. Further, we can explain the discipleship process outlined in this book: establishing relationships, engaging in spiritual dialogue, and equipping others to recycle the process.

No matter what gender you are, it is possible to disciple both men and women. The research revealed some helpful information about gender roles in making disciples. Disciples were influenced differently depending on the gender of the discipler. As figure 12.2 shows, male disciplers had an equal influence on both male and female disciples (30 percent). However, female disciplers influenced female disciples almost three times more than they influenced male disciples (29 percent as opposed to 11 percent).

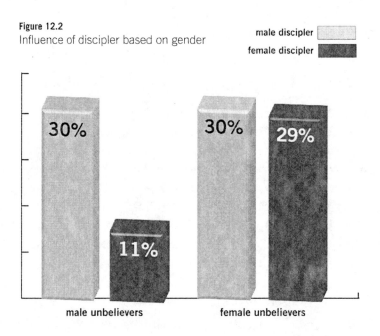

Figure 12.2
Influence of discipler based on gender

male discipler
female discipler

30%   30%   29%

11%

male unbelievers   female unbelievers

We can only surmise why female disciplers influence women more than men. Perhaps women do not view themselves as qualified as men to share the gospel. Or, it could be that women are not encouraged to share the gospel with others, and have not been given the opportunity to be adequately equipped. Regardless of the reasons, women have played a vital role in leading others to Jesus. Therefore, we should have an egalitarian approach to equipping others by not overlooking women.

Equipping others is a worthwhile endeavor. When our church initiated an equipping ministry, the participants that completed the program revealed that they were 30 percent more equipped to make disciples of others. If equipping is handled well, it trains people how to develop a personal relationship with Jesus, it gives them the knowledge they need for discipling others, and it teaches them how to fulfill the Great Commission.

When disciples have been fully equipped, churches can formally commission them to be ministers. Sometimes, this will mean being missionaries in their own communities. Other times, this will result in sending them to become church planters or missionaries to others countries.

OUR DANGEROUS CALLING

Discipleship is a dangerous calling. Jesus charges us with the incredible task of having an eternal influence on someone's soul. Not only do we have the job of developing a relationship with someone, we also have the responsibility of leading him into an intimate relationship with the Creator of the universe.

Discipleship is also a very personal endeavor. If we want to do it right, it requires us to engage in earnest soul-searching, extensive spiritual training, and personal sacrifice. It also demands that we have an intimate relationship with Jesus.

To disciple others, there are some deeply personal questions you need to ask yourself. How is your relationship with Jesus? Do you have a godly mission for your life? Does Jesus influence all your decisions? Knowing that relationships require a quantitative amount of time, are you willing to invest your time by becoming intimately involved in the lives of others? Are you threatened by questions you cannot answer, and do you have faith that God will guide you in spiritual conversations with others?

The real question is: Why are you not telling others about Jesus? If discipleship seems too complicated or too difficult for you, remember that Jesus willingly became a man and sacrificed his life for us so that we might have eternal life. Can you think of a better reason to disciple others?

Nothing about discipleship seems easy, and it is certainly not for everyone. So why do it? Why not take the easy way out and simply avoid it altogether? The answer is obvious: We are called by Jesus to make disciples. Making and equipping disciples is our reason for existing.

We can read all the books on discipleship in the world and still not lead the life of a discipler. If we truly love Jesus, and we have experienced the strength, healing, and hope that he offers, it will be difficult to keep us from sharing this good news with others. We will be compelled to shout from the rooftops, "Jesus lives! He loves you! He cares for you!"

QUESTIONS FOR DISCUSSION

- Are most of your friends unbelievers or believers? What is something you can do to expand your relationships?

- Is it difficult for you to engage in spiritual dialogue with unbelievers? Explain.

- What are some ways your church can serve the community?

- Read Galatians 5:25. What is the role of the Holy Spirit in discipleship?

- Read Ephesians 4:11–13. What are some reasons people should be equipped?

PERSONAL REFLECTION

- Are you spiritually prepared to disciple others? If not, what can you do to prepare yourself?

- Pray that God will enable you to commit yourself into a discipling relationship with another person.

13

Preparing to Live Dangerously

There is a God shaped vacuum in the heart of every man which cannot be
filled by any created thing, but only by God,
the Creator, made known through Jesus.

—Blaise Pascal

The coldest weather I ever experienced was one winter day when I was in sixth grade. The day began much like a typical school day in North Pole, Alaska. I woke up, ate breakfast, and put on my first layer of clothes. Then, to determine how many more layers of clothes to put on, I went to the living room window, cupped my hands around my face and leaned in close. This proved unproductive—it was pitch-black outside, and I could not see anything. Hoping to get a better view, I reached for a flashlight and shined the light through the window and onto our outside thermometer. I was stunned when the mercury revealed a temperature of seventy-two degrees below zero! Winters routinely dropped to sixty degrees below zero, but this was out of the ordinary. I was disturbed—not only because it was bitterly cold—but also because I would have to walk to the bus stop and wait for the bus in the frigid temperature. Schools in North Pole did not close for any reason, so avoiding the bus stop was not an option.

I grudgingly stepped outside to face the bone-chilling weather. A scarf covered my mouth to protect my lungs from directly inhaling the relentlessly penetrating cold air. Everything was still and disturbingly quiet, except for the crunching sound my boots made as I stepped on the frozen, packed snow. I looked up and noticed the ice fog was particularly thick that day, which lowered my visibility. After walking the quarter-mile lane and reaching the bus stop, I noticed that several other children were already there. We greeted each other with nods because it took too much effort to speak. After a few minutes, we heard the sound of a truck approaching. We all instinctively turned our backs to the oncoming vehicle to avoid facing the unbearable cold of the wind stream following it. Unfortunately, the vehicle was not our bus, so we were forced to continue waiting. Stomping our feet to keep warm was out of the question, because our legs and feet were too stiff to move comfortably, so we simply stood and waited for the bus.

After forty minutes of waiting in the numbing cold, it was obvious that the bus was not coming that day. Someone finally broke the silence and uttered what we all had been thinking: "What are we doing here?" That simple statement exposed the futility of continuing to stand in freezing temperatures and led to an epiphany—we must do something different! We slowly made our way to a nearby neighbor's house to warm up, but it took the rest of the day at home to thaw out.

Many of us find ourselves standing in the middle of a frozen, spirit-numbing life wondering, "What are we doing here?" "Why do I exist?" "Is there more to life than working, eating, sleeping, and dying?" We come to the realization that there must be more to life than waiting for a bus that never comes. Until we reach that point, our actions will betray the cold lifelessness of unplanned living. If we sincerely desire to lead dangerous lives, we need to act intentionally.

INTENTIONAL DISCIPLING

How do we act intentionally? By becoming like Jesus. Philippians 2:5–7 says, "Your attitude should be the same as that of Christ Jesus: Who, being in very nature God, did not consider equality with God something to be grasped, but made himself nothing, taking the very nature of a servant, being made in human likeness."

Jesus was able to relate to people because he became one of us. He willingly forfeited his power and position so he could be seen—not as an out-of-reach king—but as a fully vested human being. Jesus humbly met people on their level. As a result, he was able to establish relationships with unbelievers and intentionally disciple them.

We can have the same influence on unbelievers if we intentionally seek to relate to them. This is not accomplished by a change in outward actions, but by intentionally becoming transformed into the image of Christ. When we are a new creature, our outward actions will be a natural extension of our Christlikeness. There will be no need to pretend or perform in any way. Our lives will be dangerous, and we will lead others to Jesus!

We reflect Jesus by the characteristics we portray to others. The research revealed the characteristics of Jesus that influence unbelievers to follow him. For example, when we exhibit the characteristic of love, we influence both men and women to become followers of Jesus. However, women who demonstrate love have an even greater influence on men than women, especially when they are not related to them.

If we are related to unbelievers, we have the greatest opportunity to influence them to become disciples of Jesus. According to the data, unbelievers are influenced by family members more than any other type of relationship. Being cognizant of this challenges us to pay special attention to the needs of our relatives and friends who are unbelievers. They are natural candidates for beginning discipling relationships, because a degree of trust has already been established. We have the most influence on our relatives when we demonstrate love to them, regardless of our gender. Love is shown to others when we are accepting, compassionate, and sacrificial in our interactions with unbelievers.

Our faithfulness to God also influences unbelievers to establish a relationship with Jesus, especially if we are related to them. Faithfulness is naturally expressed to others when we are transformed into the image of Jesus. It is revealed to others when we are submissive to God, obedient to him, and when we have a mature faith.

Authenticity is another characteristic that is revealed to others when we are transformed into the image of Christ. Demonstrating authenticity in our lives has an impact on unbelievers, especially if they are men. We exhibit authenticity to others when we are genuine in our faith, transparent in our struggles, and when we are consistent in our lifestyles.

If we reflect Jesus by portraying the characteristic of knowledge, we will influence unbelievers to come to Jesus. If we are male, we have the most influence on female unbelievers by exhibiting knowledge to them. This challenges men who desire to disciple women to habitually study God's Word, make Scripture relevant, and to welcome spiritual questions with gentleness and respect.

Trustworthiness is expressed to others when we are transformed into the image of Christ. When we demonstrate trust to others, we influence them to enter into relationship with Jesus—particularly if we are men and they are women. If we are related to women who are unbelievers, we have the most influence on them when we express trustworthiness. Trust is communicated by exhibiting confidentiality, integrity, and honesty in our lives.

Care is another characteristic of Jesus that is expressed to others when we are transformed into new creatures. Demonstrating care influences unbelievers—especially women—to follow Jesus. We demonstrate care to others when we listen to them, give them our time, and when we are patient with them.

Our passion for Jesus influences unbelievers to establish a relationship with him, especially if they are male friends of ours. If we are ministers who express passion, we have the opportunity to significantly influence male unbelievers. We demonstrate passion to others when we are devoted to Jesus, speak with enthusiasm, and when we are driven to share the gospel with them.

What characteristics of Jesus do we express to others? A tool comprised of the characteristics most influential in leading unbelievers to Christ can be found in Appendix C. This instrument was created from former unbelievers' descriptions of these characteristics. This tool will help determine the degree to which we demonstrate these characteristics to others.

Although our age is not something we can control, it also plays a significant role in discipling unbelievers. In most cases, we have the most influence on others who are around our own age. These are the people we need to pay special attention to in our discipling efforts. However, as we have observed, those who are thirteen and under are most influenced by disciplers who are between twenty-nine and forty-three years of age. If we are in this age group, it is important to be aware that we have this impact on unbelievers who are thirteen and under, and act on this knowledge.

As the research has revealed, the majority of people came to Jesus because they were influenced by a one-on-one relationship with another person. This puts the burden on us to lead people to Jesus. We are the ones who must take the leadership in discipling. We need to initiate relationships with unbelievers, engage them in spiritual dialogue, and spiritually equip them to disciple others. In short, our task is to take the hand of an unbeliever and guide her every step of the way to Jesus.

God will guide our discipleship efforts. In Philippians 1:6, Paul told the church in Philippi, "he who began a good work in you will carry it on to completion until the day of Christ Jesus." God is not finished working in us; he will give us the strength, wisdom, and courage to disciple others! If we put our faith in Jesus, he will take care of everything else.

PREPARATION FOR INTENTIONAL DISCIPLESHIP

Before we can intentionally disciple unbelievers, it is crucial that we are spiritually prepared. This does not mean that we need to understand ancient Greek or have a seminary degree; intentional discipling includes the process of strengthening our own faith before we can introduce Jesus to others.

Strengthen Relationship with Jesus

Preparing ourselves spiritually means having a meaningful relationship with Jesus and expressing that affiliation through our interactions with unbelievers. One way we can build a deep relationship with Jesus is by actively engaging in spiritual disciplines that draw us close to him, such as Bible study, meditation, fasting, and prayer. Consistent exercise of these activities is critical for drawing us close to the heart of Jesus, and will enable us to share his love with others.

Our relationship with Jesus transforms us from the inside out and is manifested through our relationships with unbelievers. In other words, our discipling will be a reflection of the way Jesus discipled others. When we become like Jesus, our actions will express his characteristics. The research discovered the characteristics that had the biggest impact on leading an unbeliever to Jesus were love, faithfulness, authenticity, knowledge, trust, care, and passion. These are the discipling traits of Jesus. We may possess and demonstrate some of these traits, but not others. That is okay. As we have seen in previous chapters, unbelievers respond differently to the portrayal of characteristics based on their age, gender, or type of relationship we have with them. The vital thing to remember is that unbelievers are most influenced by us when we exhibit these characteristics. If we have an intimate relationship with Jesus, we will naturally radiate his characteristics and others will come to be in relationship with him.

Seek God's Guidance

Before we intentionally begin planting spiritual seeds, we must prepare the soil by seeking God's guidance through prayer. If we sincerely ask for God's direction and wisdom, he will lead us in the discipleship process.

About a year ago, a friend of mine asked me for advice on a family member. His relative was sick and dying, and had never given his life to Jesus. Moreover, his relative vehemently opposed Christianity, and avoided any religious discussions with disciples of Jesus. My friend asked me how he could reach this man with the gospel. I told him to pray about the situation, and trust that God would eventually provide a solution. My friend began praying for his relative and asked his believing family members to pray, also. Recently, my friend told me that his relative had decided to follow Jesus! When I asked him to tell me how that happened, he reminded me of the advice I had given him, and was convinced that prayer was the key to his relative's salvation.

God has compassion on the lost, and he will guide us as we disciple them. Prayer cannot be overstated. It prepares unbelievers for harvest. In the case of my friend's relative, God softened the hatred he harbored toward Christians most of his life, which encouraged the man to be receptive to the good news. If we know people that need Jesus, we need to ask God to work in their lives. When we seek God's guidance in prayer, he will respond in amazing ways. God still performs miracles today!

Trust Spiritual Protection

When I was a boy, preparing to spend time in the Alaskan cold was quite an ordeal. The secret to enduring the elements was dressing in layers. The first layer was underwear and socks followed by thermal underwear and socks. Then we put on outer clothes of pants and a long-sleeved shirt. Snow pants and a heavy jacket with a drawstring and hood were worn over the clothes. Before we could put our feet in boots, we had to wrap them in plastic bags and tie them off with rubber bands to keep our feet dry. On our hands, we wore gloves over glove liners. To finish the ensemble, we wore a scarf around our neck and a woolen hat or ski mask, depending on the severity of the cold. The difficulty in dressing was trying to cover every possible opening where the outside air could enter. If we did not have adequate protection from the bitter cold, we would literally freeze.

Just as we need to take steps to protect ourselves from freezing temperatures, when we live dangerously, we need to be prepared for the harsh difficulties that will inevitably attack us. First Peter 5:8 tells us that "the devil prowls around like a roaring lion looking for someone to devour." Satan will do everything he can to thwart our thorough preparations and efforts to live dangerously, but Jesus does not leave us in the cold without appropriate gear. In John 16:33 Jesus promised, "In this world you will have trouble. But take heart! I have overcome the world." We can be confident that when we face struggles, the most powerful being in the universe is protecting us. Just as proper clothing protected me from severely cold weather, protection from hardships depends on how we clothe ourselves. When we trust Jesus to cover us with his protective arms, we do not need to be afraid of living dangerously.

THE CHARGE TO LIVE DANGEROUSLY

One of the greatest lessons of life is highlighted in the film, *The Shawshank Redemption*. Andy Dufresne, the main character, ends up in prison for a crime he did not commit. At the climax of the movie, Andy tells his friend Red, "It all comes down to a simple choice: Get busy living or get busy dying." Red spends a sleepless night fearing that Andy would commit suicide. However, in the morning, Andy is missing from his cell. During the night, he grabbed life by the horns and escaped from Shawshank Prison! His decisively bold action radically alters the rest of his life.

Like Andy, you also have a choice to make: You can take a laissez-faire approach and ignore those who are bound by sin, or you can intentionally guide them to the one who can set them free. What would happen if no one was busy living the Great Commission? The next generation would grow up not knowing God! It is dangerous not to seek and save the lost. You have a mission on earth, and only a short time to complete it. There are no guarantees that you—or others—will be here tomorrow, but tomorrow will come whether you are ready or not! Be so captivated by the grace of Jesus that you cannot help but live dangerously!

Jesus said, "The harvest is plentiful, but the workers are few" (Matt 9:37). Jesus is calling you to plant spiritual seeds that lead to a bountiful harvest. Are you ready to answer the call? What are you waiting for? Now is the time to ignite a fire in your belly for making disciples! You are the key to intentionally establishing relationships with unbelievers, and leading them into an eternal relationship with Jesus. Live dangerously!

QUESTIONS FOR DISCUSSION

- Who is the most influential person you have known? How did he or she live intentionally?

- Read Philippians 2:5–7. What can we learn from the example of Jesus?

- Which characteristics of intentional disciplers do you demonstrate the most to others? Which characteristics do you need to improve?

- How can you spiritually prepare yourself for discipling others?

- Read Matthew 9:37. How does this verse apply to your life?

PERSONAL REFLECTION

- Are you living dangerously? If not, what steps can you take to change your life?

- In Matthew 9:38, Jesus says, "Ask the Lord of the harvest, therefore, to send out workers into his harvest field." Pray that God will use you as a worker that will glorify him.

Appendix A

Research Instrument

1. What state do you live in?

- ALABAMA
- ALASKA
- ARIZONA
- ARKANSAS
- CALIFORNIA
- COLORADO
- CONNECTICUT
- DELAWARE
- FLORIDA
- GEORGIA
- HAWAII
- IDAHO
- ILLINOIS
- INDIANA
- IOWA
- KANSAS
- KENTUCKY
- LOUISIANA
- MAINE
- MARYLAND
- MASSACHUSETTS
- MICHIGAN
- MINNESOTA
- MISSISSIPPI
- MISSOURI
- MONTANA

- NEBRASKA
- NEVADA
- NEW HAMPSHIRE
- NEW JERSEY
- NEW MEXICO
- NEW YORK
- NORTH CAROLINA
- NORTH DAKOTA
- OHIO
- OKLAHOMA
- OREGON
- PENNSYLVANIA
- RHODE ISLAND
- SOUTH CAROLINA
- SOUTH DAKOTA
- TENNESSEE
- TEXAS
- UTAH
- VERMONT
- VIRGINIA
- WASHINGTON
- WEST VIRGINIA
- WISCONSIN
- WYOMING
- Outside of U.S.

2. What is your age?

   - 13 or younger
   - 14–28
   - 29–43
   - 44–62
   - 63 or older

3. What is your gender?

   - Male
   - Female

4. Was there someone who was especially influential in leading you to Jesus?

   - Yes
   - No

The following questions are about the person who was the most influential in leading you to Jesus:

5. What gender is the person who was influential in leading you to Jesus?
    - Male
    - Female

6. What was the age of this person when you gave your life to Jesus?
    - 13 or younger
    - 14-28
    - 29-43
    - 44-62
    - 63 or older

7. What was your relationship with this person when you first met?

    Relative
    Neighbor
    Friend
    Coworker
    Other _____

8. How long did you know this person before Jesus came up in conversation?
    - 0-3 months
    - 3-6 months
    - 6 months to a year
    - More than a year

9. Which one of you was the first to bring up Jesus in conversation after you met?

    You
    The other person

10. Why did you feel comfortable discussing spiritual matters with this person?

11. How long was it from the time Jesus first came up in conversation with this person until you gave your life to Him?

> 0-3 months
> 3-6 months
> 6 months to a year
> More than a year

12. Which one of this person's character traits had the biggest impact on your decision to give your life to Jesus?

> Accepting
> Authentic
> Bold
> Caring
> Courageous
> Faithful
> Forgiving
> Gentle
> Giving
> Good
> Humble
> Joyful
> Kind
> Knowledgeable
> Loving
> Passionate
> Patient
> Peaceful
> Self-controlled
> Trustworthy
> Other _____

13. Give an example of how this person was accepting, authentic, etc.

Appendix B

Research Method

A RESEARCH STUDY WAS conducted with an online survey from January to April of 2009. A random sampling method was used. The sample size consisted of 1,436 respondents from 49 states. Data were described by frequencies and cross-tabulated using Chi-square. All correlations included in the analyses were determined to be statistically significant with at least 95 percent confidence.

The Characteristics Indicator in Appendix C was tested for internal consistency using Chronbachs Alpha, and was determined to have an average coefficient of over .70, which indicates good internal reliability.

Appendix C

Characteristics Indicator

Instructions

Indicate the degree to which the following statements are true of you using the scale below.

1 = never
2 = rarely
3 = sometimes
4 = very often
5 = always

1. I accept others for who they are		1	2	3	4	5
2. I trust God no matter what happen		1	2	3	4	5
3. I am a patient person		1	2	3	4	5
4. I am prepared to study the Bible with others		1	2	3	4	5
5. I am truthful with others		1	2	3	4	5
6. I communicate sincerity to others		1	2	3	4	5
7. I express the joy Jesus has given me		1	2	3	4	5
8. I am a good listener		1	2	3	4	5
9. I am willing to help others in need		1	2	3	4	5
10. I can make the Bible relevant to others		1	2	3	4	5
11. I know that God is working in my life		1	2	3	4	5
12. I can admit my weaknesses to others		1	2	3	4	5
13. I feel driven to share Jesus with others		1	2	3	4	5

14. I keep my word   1   2   3   4   5

15. I have a hunger for seeking and saving the lost   1   2   3   4   5

16. I look for ways to serve others   1   2   3   4   5

17. I seek God's guidance in prayer   1   2   3   4   5

18. I consistently read the Bible   1   2   3   4   5

19. I can keep others' secrets to myself   1   2   3   4   5

20. I am a genuine person   1   2   3   4   5

21. I am concerned with the wellbeing of others   1   2   3   4   5

22. I am an encourager   1   2   3   4   5

23. I am not afraid to talk to others about Jesus   1   2   3   4   5

24. I have a personal relationship with Jesus   1   2   3   4   5

25. I can back up my beliefs with biblical facts   1   2   3   4   5

26. I am real   1   2   3   4   5

27. I willingly give my time to others   1   2   3   4   5

28. I am dependable   1   2   3   4   5

29. I am able to use the Word to teach others   1   2   3   4   5

30. I express my enthusiasm for Jesus   1   2   3   4   5

31. I know that God is with me during hard times   1   2   3   4   5

32. I am honest with others   1   2   3   4   5

33. I am transparent with others   1   2   3   4   5

34. I am attentive when others are speaking to me   1   2   3   4   5

35. I consider the needs of others   1   2   3   4   5

Scoring

Total the numbers in each column. *The highest totals are the characteristics you demonstrate the most. The lowest totals are the characteristics you show the least.*

	Total	
1, 9, 16, 22, 35	____	Love
2, 11, 17, 24, 31	____	Faith
6, 12, 20, 26, 33	____	Authenticity
4, 10, 18, 25, 29	____	Knowledge
5, 14, 19, 28, 32	____	Trustworthy
3, 8, 21, 27, 34	____	Caring
7, 13, 15, 23, 30	____	Passionate

Bibliography

Barna, George. "Evangelism Is Most Effective Among Kids." No Pages. Online: *http://www .barna.org/barna-update/article/5-barna-update/196-evangelism-is-most-effective -among-kids* (October 11, 2004).

Barna, George. *The Habits of Highly Effective Churches*. Ventura: Regal, 1999.

Carson, D. A. *The Expositor's Bible Commentary*. Grand Rapids: Zondervan, 1984.

Cook, F. C. *The Speaker's Commentary on the New Testament*. New York: Charles Scribner, 1886.

Elwell, Walter A. *Commentary of the Bible*. Grand Rapids: Baker, 1989.

Herodotus. *The Histories*. 4. Translated by A. D. Godley. Cambridge: Harvard University Press, 1920.

Keysar, Ariela, and Kosmin, Barry A. *"American Religious Identification Survey."* No pages. Online: *http://www.americanreligionsurvey-aris.org/reports/ARIS_Report_2008.pdf.*

Rainer, Thom. *Surprising Insights from the Unchurched*. Grand Rapids: Zondervan, 2001.

Warneck, Gustav. *Evangelische Missionslehre: ein missionstheoretischer versuch*. 3 vols. Gotha: F. A. Perthes, 1897.

Scripture Index